Writing Women in Central America

This series of publications on Africa, Latin America, Southeast Asia, and Global and Comparative Studies is designed to present significant research, translation, and opinion to area specialists and to a wide community of persons interested in world affairs. The editor seeks manuscripts of quality on any subject and can usually make a decision regarding publication within three months of receipt of the original work. Production methods generally permit a work to appear within one year of acceptance. The editor works closely with authors to produce a high-quality book. The series appears in a paperback format and is distributed worldwide. For more information, contact the executive editor at Ohio University Press, Scott Quadrangle, University Terrace, Athens, Ohio 45701.

Executive editor: Gillian Berchowitz
AREA CONSULTANTS
Africa: Diane M. Ciekawy
Latin America: Thomas Walker
Southeast Asia: William H. Frederick
Global and Comparative Studies: Ann R. Tickamyer

The Ohio University Research in International Studies series is published for the Center for International Studies by Ohio University Press. The views expressed in individual volumes are those of the authors and should not be considered to represent the policies or beliefs of the Center for International Studies, Ohio University Press, or Ohio University.

Writing Women in Central America

Gender and the Fictionalization of History

Laura Barbas-Rhoden

Ohio University Research in International Studies
Latin America Series No. 41
Ohio University Press
Athens

12 11 10 09 08 07 06 05 04 03   5 4 3 2 1

The books in the Ohio University Research in International Studies Series
are printed on acid-free paper ∞

Permission has been granted by the editors of the following journals to reprint those
portions of the text that have appeared in earlier form in their publications:

"The Quest for the Mother in the Novels of Gioconda Belli." *Letras femininas*
26.1–2 (2000): 81–97.

"Colonial Realities and Fictional Truths in the Narratives of Tatiana Lobo." *Hispanófila* 137 (2003): 127–40.

"*Calypso* en la modernidad: contrapuntos y respuestas." Trans. Sergio Gómez Atencio. *Revista Comunicación* [Cartago, Costa Rica] 12.23 (November 2002): 73–79.

Library of Congress Cataloging-in-Publication

Barbas-Rhoden, Laura, 1974–
    Writing women in Central America : gender and the fictionalization of history
/ Laura Barbas-Rhoden.
        p.   cm. — (Ohio University research in international studies. Latin
America series ; no. 41)
    Includes bibliographical references and index.
    ISBN 0-89680-233-7 (pbk. : alk. paper)
    1. Central American fiction—Women authors—History and criticism.
2. Central American fiction—20th century—History and criticism.
3. Literature and history—Central America.   4. Women in literature.
5. Alegría, Claribel—Criticism and interpretation.   6. Aguilar, Rosario,
1938—Criticism and interpretation.   7. Belli, Gioconda, 1948—Criticism and
interpretation.   8. Lobo, Tatiana—Criticism and interpretation.
I. Title.   II. Research in international studies. Latin America series ; no. 41.

PQ7471.5.B37   2003
863'.6099287'09728—dc21   2003051714

For my parents,
Who taught me of justice and of peace.

Contents

Acknowledgments

I am indebted to many people for insight, advice, and encouragement in this project. I thank Maureen Shea and Nicasio Urbina for opening the doors of Central American literature to me. I am also grateful for the help of Félix Bolaños, Teresa Soufas, and the staff of the Stone Center for Latin American Studies and the Latin American Library at Tulane University.

Many colleagues provided me with information and camaraderie, and I especially thank a number of women for their solidarity. Ana Yolanda Contreras, Daniela Flesler, Susan Griswold, Catherine Lerat Schmitz, Emma Matute, and Anne Rodrick shared with me books, materials, and ideas, and I thank them for those, as well as for their moral support.

I also owe a tremendous debt to the authors included in this study, some of whom graciously provided their time and insights during my travels to Central America. The Mellon Foundation and the Stone Center at Tulane University provided funding for my first projects in Central America, during which I met a number of the authors included in these pages. Wofford College gave me support for writing and revision, and I thank Dean Dan Maultsby and my colleagues for their vote of confidence in this work. I am also grateful to the staff at Ohio University Press for their conscientious and thoughtful assistance in preparing the manuscript.

Finally, I thank my husband, Rob, who served as thesaurus, proofreader, and constant companion throughout this process. His solidarity helped make the preparation of the project a joy.

Introduction

"Disrupting the Thread"

Dominant Narratives and the Works of Central American Women

[T]he critic must attempt to fully realize, and take responsibility for, the unspoken, unrepresented pasts that haunt the historical present.
—Homi K. Bhabha, *The Location of Culture*

WEAPONS, PLOTS, VIOLENCE. Lush landscapes and guerrillas. Central America is a site of danger (again), but not because of its revolutions. The danger is in words—the words of women.

In their texts, women have taken up arms, spun plots, uncovered violence. They have reinvented landscapes and histories. They have threatened identities, politics, and social structures. My project is about their reinterpretations, about the world as they have seen it as women, citizens, artists. Most particularly, it is about the "dangerous supplements" to history that they have offered through their fictionalizations of the past.[1]

Contrary to the beliefs some have tenaciously held, neither Central America nor women are inherently dangerous. In the global designs of empires and the twisted logic of patriarchal myths, they have been assigned these identities. In the last decades of the twentieth

1

century, the protests against these identities became a clamor. Women and indigenous peoples, in particular, confronted and contested the roles they had been assigned.

My narrative concerns four women from Central America. They are the innovators to whom I refer—Claribel Alegría, Gioconda Belli, Rosario Aguilar, and Tatiana Lobo. During the last third of the twentieth century, they produced more than a dozen books in which they have remembered the "unspoken, unrepresented pasts" (Bhabha, 12) that haunt the present. Theirs are the words that are dangerous. With them, they offer fictionalizations of the past, bending genre categories and blurring the line between history and fiction.

The authors have taken history, sized it up, and found it lacking. Proposing to supplement, to append, to account for their own existences, they tell other stories in dangerous supplements to the historical record. Speaking what has previously been unspoken, the writers comment on history and replace it with a new vision of the past. Their historical narratives threaten traditional history, as well as the nations and identities founded upon it. They start by confronting the marginalization and denial of memories of certain groups (mostly women and indigenous peoples) in history. In doing so, the writers reveal that history is contingent upon the priorities and values of the historian. Like them, traditional historians have spoken from a particular time, place, and culture, but unlike them, they have erased the marks from their discourse. In adding supplements to stories told about the past, numerous women authors remind us that history always belongs to someone. It does not have the objectivity it has claimed, and it can be questioned. Since, in Central America, history has carried enormous weight in the construction of national identity, supplementing is a dangerous move. It threatens not just the past but also the present and the future.

In the retelling of history, Alegría, Belli, Aguilar, and Lobo challenge the accepted order of life in the isthmus. They also question the logic that justifies that order. They expose the politics behind divisions such as elite/popular and literature/orality, and they bring into focus gendered dichotomies like public/private, passive/active, desired/desiring, which have been inscribed in the story of the past. This act, too, is menacing, for as Djelal Kadir writes, "Nothing threatens . . . claims [of representational mastery and interpretive authority] as much as the cultural economy of otherness because alterity interjects a wild card, an ideological indeterminacy that potentially remands any position . . . dislocating territorialization from its privileged center, unmasking the discourse of self-justification, and disrupting the thread, the line of the dominant narrative" (6). The Others of Central America have long possessed an oral tradition that appropriates and subverts representations mobilized by hegemonic culture; the contemporary performance of *El güegüense* in Masaya, Nicaragua, is but one example of this tradition.[2]

Drawing upon a long collective memory of resistance, recent interventions contest the powerful not just through the famous (and famously stereotyped) revolutions, but also through forms such as the novel. And when the marginalized women, indigenous peoples, and Africans began to *write* their own stories, they did not just blindly assume a Western cultural tradition along with other trappings of modernity. Rather, they appropriated the novel to disrupt the flow of the dominant narrative from within, uncovering its "discourse of self-justification" by telling their own stories. This is significant because more often than not Latin American writers have worked in the service of the privileged. Close to the powerful, scribes penned the documents that invented empires and made republics. Only recently has the writer become the critic of social injustices and memory of alternative realities, and she has told other stories.

Confluences: Women, Books, and Politics in Latin America

The revolutionary movements of Central America and the boom of publications by Latin American women are two frequently discussed phenomena that concern my treatment of women's writing. On the Central American front, revolutionary upheavals and the artistic exuberance they sparked began a new cultural boom. Expressions of that boom included primitivist painting, *exteriorista* poetry, and the testimonial and documentary novel.[3] Associated with leftist movements in ascendance from the late 1960s until the signing of peace accords in Guatemala and El Salvador in the 1990s, the works and their creators attracted large audiences and numerous critical studies. Innovative techniques, recourse to oral traditions, and acute social consciousness characterized works that garnered worldwide acclaim for their artistic merit and political engagement.

Furthermore, Central American artists were given an important platform by solidarity groups worldwide. Renowned authors traveled internationally, disseminating art and information, among them Ernesto Cardenal, Sergio Ramírez, Manlio Argueta, Roque Dalton, Roberto Sosa, and the testimonial narrators Rigoberta Menchú and Omar Cabezas. Testimonial literature, in particular, emerged as witness to a collective struggle, gaining prominence with works like Menchú's 1984 testimony, *Me llamo Rigoberta Menchú y así me nació la conciencia.* This is by far the most prominent and controversial Latin American text in the genre.[4] Other important works appeared in conjunction with the Salvadoran and Nicaraguan revolutionary movements, such as Argueta's pseudotestimony *Un día en la vida* (1980) and Cabezas's *La montaña es algo más que una inmensa estepa verde* (1982).

Just as authors portrayed the reality of the isthmus in their texts, amateur and professional artists gave Central American landscapes and life value in primitivist painting and exteriorist poetry. Like the testimonial, exteriorist writing and primitivist art emphasized collective memories and local knowledge, communicated without artifice in forms accessible to the "common people." One of the most prominent cultural leaders among the Nicaraguan revolutionaries, Ernesto Cardenal became an important advocate of these expressions, pro-

4

moting them among peasants in the Solentiname community and later as minister of culture in the Sandinista administration (Whisnant, 185-86).[5]

The boom of testimonial literature and revolutionary poetry sparked in international audiences an unprecedented interest in Central American literature. According to some, however, this was only a momentary flash of enthusiasm that gave way to a relative decline in the distribution and study of Central American texts. Guatemalan novelist and critic Arturo Arias, for instance, observes, "Entre 1978 y 1990 Centroamérica logró, a un altísimo costo, que el mundo se fijara en ella. Pero ya en los años noventa, pareciera como si volviéramos a la situación de antaño. Centroamérica ... sigue importando poco, y a pocos, en la esfera cultural" ("Descolonizando," 74) [Between 1978 and 1990, Central America managed, at an extremely high cost, to gain the world's attention. But now, in the 1990s, it seems as if we have returned to the same situation as before. Central America ... continues to matter very little, and to very few, in the world of culture]. In an effort to highlight outstanding texts from the region, Arias published another article entitled "Conciencia de la palabra," in which he compiled a list of important contributors to Central American literature since the 1970s (50). Strikingly, of the nineteen novels Arias identified as part of the *nueva narrativa centroamericana* (new Central American narrative), only one—*El último juego* (1977) by Panamanian Gloria Guardia—was penned by a woman. If Central America matters very little and to very few, women writing in Central America appear to have mattered even less, even in studies whose exclusive focus is on the literature of the region.[6]

Publications and translations since the appearance of Arias's two articles reveal that Central American literature is gaining attention once again, though it is necessary to look among the women writers to note that change. In fact, in the last three decades it has increasingly been women writers who have contributed narrative innovations and practiced cultural criticism through their fictions. The authors I study here, for example, not only examine political reality in their texts (as do other authors concerned with social justice), they also question the human social arrangement at its most basic levels: the relations between men and women; the nature of roles assigned according to gender; and the place of women and other marginalized people in the memory of the modern state.

This brings us to the second phenomenon of late-twentieth-century Latin America: the explosion of bestsellers by women. In Latin America as in other parts of the world, the few women who have had public lives have generally appeared as isolated "cases" of genius, prowess, or ability. Furthermore, women of historical import such as the seventeenth-century poet Sor Juana Inés de la Cruz, were often associated with aberration.[7] As women's history pioneer Gerda Lerner suggests, actually relating the story of the margins implies a radical overhaul not only of notions of history but also of nation, identity, and culture, all of which are predicated upon interpretations of the past.[8]

Fortunately, the world has changed since the time of Sor Juana. Prompted by the women's movement in Latin America, social transformations gradually permitted the entrance of more women into the literary world from the 1960s onward. Subsequent decades saw more publications of woman-authored texts, some of which achieved the status of bestsellers in the 1980s and 1990s. In fact, women may have outstripped men after the Boom.[9] Some observers have suggested that the extraordinarily popular *La casa de los espíritus* (1982) and *Como agua para chocolate* (1989), by Isabel Allende and Laura Esquivel respectively, may now be more familiar to the reading (and viewing) public than Gabriel García Márquez's *Cien años de soledad* (1967), the most famous text of the Latin American Boom (Franco "Afterword", 226).

Categorized by some as "literatura light," Latin American bestsellers by Mexican and Southern Cone women demonstrate a complex imbrication of social processes linked to neoliberal reform and globalization. Neoliberal policies first took hold in Mexico and the Southern Cone in the 1970s under governments that were at best unrepresentative. The trends there were quite distinct from those on-going in Central America at the same time.[10] With a solidly established publishing industry, Mexico and the Southern Cone have also been the sources of the bestsellers of the 1980s and 1990s, by authors such as Angeles Mastretta (Mexico), Sara Sefchovich (Mexico), Marcela Serrano (Chile), and Isabel Allende (Chile). Memoirs and pseudomemoirs figure prominently among their works, which feature almost exclusively female protagonists who are educated, middle-class wives or mothers frustrated with the tedium of daily life and in search of self-fulfillment.

On one hand, the success of these books in Latin America is a powerful statement about women's seizure of the word in order to construct their own worlds. On the other hand, the plots generally feature a process of *concientización* (consciousness raising) that results in changes that are personal or domestic. Rarely is there any radical social critique or transformation, as in the concientización of testimonial literature. Novels such as Sefchovich's *La señora de los sueños* (1993), Serrano's *Antigua vida mía* (1995), and Mastretta's *Mal de amores* (1996) all conclude with a re-establishment of the social order, which has not been overhauled but rather modified slightly in the immediate vicinity of the female protagonist, who sought change.

If one considers the plots of many bestsellers in relation to neo-liberal policies, a disquieting complicity becomes evident. Official economic policies in Mexico and the Southern Cone since the 1970s have advocated open markets, monetary reform, and the privatization of everything imaginable. They have also opened the door to con-sumerism, emphasizing peace and prosperity, the maintenance of the status quo, and the gradual improvement of life through free-market reform. Concurrently, in the bestselling novels of many authors (se-lected, of course, by publishing houses with a financial stake in the venture), there is a tendency to distance the plots from macropolitical occurrences, as well as political injustice of the recent past. The focus is on a personal, intimate, and individual world where the conclusions are romantic rather than socially transformative.[11]

In contrast to these mainstream plots, those crafted by Central American women have overwhelmingly been contestatory, given to historical commentary and social critique. For that reason, while I consider the works of Alegría, Belli, Aguilar, and Lobo a part of a general explosion of women's writing, I note that the terms of their participation have been quite different. The texts of Central American women have lacked the efficient distribution that others have enjoyed; they have told stories that, because of their contestatory nature, did not always find ready patrons in institutions focused on profit. In a region that has lacked global economic importance, adequate state funding, and the mechanisms to distribute texts effectively, Central American authors have traditionally relied on informal methods of distribution. The only exception to this would be testimonial literature, which was catapulted onto the world scene by widespread international opposition to the policies of the Reagan administration in Central America.

Cultural Legacies and Central American Women

The most widely published Central American women novelists of the twentieth century are the four I include here: Claribel Alegría, Rosario Aguilar, Gioconda Belli, and Tatiana Lobo. Like their compatriots Ernesto Cardenal, Sergio Ramírez, and Manlio Argueta, these women have sought to appropriate and reclaim the traditions, oral history, and cultural legacy of the isthmus in their prose and poetry. They have produced texts that redefine contemporary reality by recovering the past. They have done so, however, from a woman-centered, often feminist perspective, and their fictional interventions in the story of modernity are the subject of my study.[12]

The expressions of Alegría, Belli, Aguilar, and Lobo are unique articulations of growing challenges to dominant narratives in Latin

America. In Latin America, the fissures and ruptures of national projects became increasingly evident first under dictatorial rule and then in the neoliberal wake that followed the defeat of the Left. As novelists and cultural critics, the authors I study have participated in the revision of national narratives that has occurred in conjunction with revolutionary movements and the social fallout of free-market reforms.[13] In cultural terms, Gustavo Pellón sees this revisionary movement as a defining characteristic of post-Boom narrative: "To illustrate by means of analogy, one could say that what the novelists of the 1970's and 1980's have tried to do is to retell *Cien años de soledad* but from the viewpoint of Mauricio Babilonia, or Pilar Ternera, or Petra Cotes, rather than from the viewpoint of the oligarchy represented (however charmingly) by the Buendía family" (280). No longer interested primarily in the Buendías of the region, post-Boom authors have turned toward sites of difference and resistance in their fictions. As latent epistemological violence and social injustice gave way to the brutal violence of repressive regimes, particularly in Central America, dissenters began to come forward en masse to tell their own stories and point out the incongruities of modernity.

Women writers not only responded to blatant political injustices but also pointed out the continuing legacy of patriarchal rules that have shaped reality on a daily basis. They signaled in fiction what Lisa Lowe and David Lloyd have commented in criticism: "Patriarchal definitions of gender are continuously reproduced throughout a genealogy of social formations: patriarchy is consistently dominant, though not identically so, under colonial rule, in nationalist regimes, and in postcolonial and neocolonial state formations" (20). As they criticized contemporary social structures, writers responded to centuries of cultural traditions, firmly rooted in the literature of nation formation and regional identity.

For Latin American nations, regional identity harks back to colonial experience and the early national period. Some understanding of this past is necessary if one is to understand how women "disrupt the

9

thread" of its emplotment. Colonial life for Spanish America began with Columbus's 1492 voyage and lasted until the independence of all but the Caribbean colonies in the 1820s. The colonial era produced an enduring social structure that privileged those of European descent and relegated indigenous populations and their cultures to a much denigrated and heavily regulated status. Upper classes accumulated large landholdings in the colonial period, and thereby altered the physical and human landscapes of the lands indigenous peoples inhabited (Woodward, 54–55). Though racial mixing was common, purity of lineage was extremely important for the wealthy, who wished to preserve territorial claims through inheritance. Thus, women of rich families were regulated by church and crown because of their reproductive capacities.

Despite the enormous importance of the colonial era, however, critics often point to the early national period and modernism as foundational moments in the construction of Latin American identity. An intellectual and artistic movement of the late nineteenth century, modernism occurred at a crucial time as the postindependence wars began to fizzle. It became the chief expression of the new republics, which for the first time presented themselves to their own citizens and other countries as nations.

The decades of war after independence had pitted conservatives against liberals in many Latin American nations. The two main political groups differed widely in their approaches toward government but little in their exclusion of women and indigenous peoples. Reactionary and paternalistic, conservatives predominated in Central America in the middle of the nineteenth century. Many held that indigenous peoples had received better treatment under the colonial system, and in 1839 in Guatemala, conservatives decreed an Indian Code, which required labor but gave indigenous peoples some protection in their land claims (Woodward, 115).

By contrast, liberals had a Westernizing mission and sought to organize land, labor, and capital to inaugurate a new economic and political order (Williams, 251). Integration into the world market justified the repression of indigenous symbolic systems, equated with backwardness and not with the progress liberals coveted. Enjoying prominence in the last three decades of the century in Central America, liberal leaders hoped that indigenous populations "would eventually be symbolically whitened" through education and integration into the national economy (Franco, *Plotting Women*, 79). In places like El Salvador, cultural "whitening" was predicated upon violence directed against the "backward" indigenous groups, whose lands were expropriated to facilitate the integration of the region into the world economy (Dunkerley, 160).

For women, a national discourse that privileged racial purity, secular education, and progress resulted in their confinement primarily to reproductive roles within the home. For liberal thinkers, the home was imagined to be a refuge from the vagaries of politics and war, and it was up to women to make it a retreat for men. Jean Franco notes,

> Women were especially crucial to the imagined community as mothers of the new men and as guardians of private life, which from Independence onward was increasingly seen as a shelter from political turmoil. Two aspects of the recodification of gender deserve special attention; the carving out of a territory of domestic stability and decency from which all low elements were expelled, and the displacement of the religious onto the national, which once again made "purity" the responsibility of women. (*Plotting Women*, 81)

In such a way, then, women became part of a project of national consolidation in tightly scripted roles: they were to be wives and mothers responsible for preserving the patriotic ideal.

Into this milieu, the modernist movement was born in Latin America. In Central America, liberal policies brought temporary economic success through agricultural exports like coffee. Modernist poets like Nicaraguan Rubén Darío indirectly benefited from an increasing wealth that fed the growth of papers, journals, and international travel. Located firmly at the center of the modernist movement, Darío was the emissary of a region confident in its new identity, as well as its ability to navigate the future with success.[14] The importance of modernism for the region was great; in fact, Stephen Tapscott holds that "Modernism was the first Latin American literary movement that spoke through and for Latin American writers identified *as* Latin Americans, citizens neither of a colony nor of separate emergent nations" (8).

However, if modernism established cultural pride and identity during the era of fin-de-siècle prosperity, it was also an ethnic and gender-specific phenomenon, not to mention a class-based one. Modernism codified and perpetuated certain gender stereotypes that persist even today. For example, Aníbal González has noted that the modernist preoccupation with style inevitably found its expression in an erotic metaphor. According to her, "En este sistema metafórico, el acto de escribir se equipara a una fecundación, en la que el cálamo o *stilus* masculino penetra y mancilla la blancura virginal de la página. Dentro de este 'romance familiar' . . . de la literatura . . . la obra literaria nace de unas nupcias en las que la voluntad ordenadora, masculina, del estilo, somete a su código al ser rebelde, desbordante y femenino de la escritura en su estado burdo, caótico, natural" (137) [In this metaphorical system, the act of writing is equated with a fertilization in which the masculine stalk or stylus penetrates and stains the virginal whiteness of the page. In this "family romance" . . . of literature . . . the literary text is born from a marriage in which the masculine will to order of the stylus, submits to its code the rebellious, excessive, and feminine nature of writing in its coarse, chaotic, and natural state]. In the code of modernism, the act of writing is gendered masculine, the passive page or chaotic natural force that must be subjected by the male imagination is gendered female, and the work of art is born from this union or violation. Similarly in the national rhetoric of the nineteenth century, the nation is gendered female, in need of male domination to realize her potential. Sexual metaphors abounded in modernist poems and in the national romances of the nineteenth century, as Doris Sommer points out in *Foundational Fictions* (1991). Within the confines of the modernist aesthetic, there was little place for metaphorical maneuvering by women writers.

Subsequent women writers like Alfonsina Storni and Gabriela Mistral broke abruptly with the modernist aesthetic, reappropriating the female body and finding new space for expression in the urban-centered, avant-garde movements in Latin America. Nevertheless, the notion of the page/nation as a space for masculine inscription has recurred throughout much of the twentieth century. It has encountered revision only in recent years, when significant numbers of writers have begun to question plots and modify allegories to make space for different expressions. In the texts considered here, for example, women are neither the object (the virginal blank page) nor the obstacle (the chaos to be subdued), but subjects and articulators of history.

When Claribel Alegría began her publishing career, the Boom was still producing the same masculinist metaphors it inherited from the colonial era and modernism. Like modernism, the Boom was a seminal movement in Latin America with international repercussions and a lasting impact on the literary community. Born in the wake of Cuban revolutionary triumph and the euphoria of sympathetic intellectuals, the Boom exported a new vision of Latin America to the world. It also shaped Latin Americans' perceptions of their own history. As Randolph Pope notes, key authors such as Carlos Fuentes, Gabriel García Márquez, and Mario Vargas Llosa "questioned traditional history and sought to replace it with . . . a more hesitant, shaded, and distrustful one" (226). They did so by employing innovative narratives that were complex and did not follow the linear plots of their realist school predecessors. However, Pellón notes, "Although written by politically liberal and leftist authors, the novels of the Boom were written from the social perspective of the center. Male authors of the middle and upper class predominate among the writers of the Boom" (280). Though they questioned history, especially as it had been told by their literary precursors and modern states, they generally did not question gender stereotypes or assumptions. As they redefined literary standards for modernity, Boom authors wrote other stories of the nation, but the stories were male-authored, male-centered, and firmly located in the urban middle and upper classes.

Like the Boom novels, the narratives of historical fiction by Alegría, Belli, Aguilar, and Lobo actively engage the turbulent past of Latin America. Unlike them, they are woman-centered. In appropriating key historical moments, the authors disrupt narratives of imperial and national success from the time of Conquest through the beginning of the twenty-first century. They do so to make room for women. They dialogue with conquistadors, scribes, and ecclesiastical authorities, men like Hernán Cortés, Pedro de Alvarado, Gonzálo Fernández de Oviedo, and Diego de Landa. What is more, these women writers extrapolate other possible histories from the silences of the texts these men wrote. They unmask the nineteenth-century narratives of liberal progress and paternalistic conservatism and reveal hidden motives in the shaping of modern nations. In revising the story of the twentieth century (when various movements attempted the dismantling and reconstruction of these nations), they unmask the idiosyncrasies in democratic progress, expose the brutality of dictatorship and the legacy of internal colonization, and reveal the shortcomings of even the leftist movements with which they have often expressed solidarity.

In 1966, Claribel Alegría began the disruption; she published her first novel. My study begins with that publication, at a time when Central America was embarking on three decades of war. It ends at the dawn of the new millennium in the globalized world of post–Cold War modernity. What came in between (and what may come after) is the subject of the following chapters.

Chapter 1

Awakening Women in Central America

Claribel Alegría's Fictions

> In the literature of civil war. . . . we may see how authors explore the
> gendering of political discourse; not only voices but political attitudes
> are encoded as masculine and feminine, and it is not unusual to find
> that female figures serve to criticize established political ideology.
> —Margaret R. Higonnet, "Civil Wars and Sexual Territories"

THROUGH HER FICTIONS and poetry, Claribel Alegría has made an
important contribution to the literature of liberation in Central America. Furthermore, her dual focus on "civil wars and sexual territories"
revised the terms of the struggle to address gender-based inequities
as well as political ones. Her writing spans several decades, during
which armed struggle emerged in El Salvador and Nicaragua and
brought the region to the forefront of international attention.[1] Similarly, Alegría's writing has carried women's stories to the center of the
dialogue about contemporary Central American social problems and
the history of injustice that has imbricated such problems in even the
most basic human relationships.

Composed and published during a period of widespread popular
unrest and government repression, Alegría's texts engage both the

reality of political oppression and the rhetoric that has configured it. She actively counters the Cold War rhetoric of the Salvadoran military regime and the Reagan administration, and she posits an alternative representation of the Central American struggles. In particular, her narrative fictionalizations of Salvadoran history point to the underlying oppression of women in society, as well as their awakenings to limitations and their subsequent insistence on change. The texts fill silences in unique ways, bending the genre of the novel toward the testimonial and the diary in order to piece together the history of women in the struggle for personal and national liberation. Both personal and political, her stories articulate the grievances not only of *el pueblo* (the common people) in general but also of women who have found themselves subjugated no matter what their social or economic circumstances.

Occasionally publishing in collaboration with her North American husband, Darwin Flakoll, Alegría challenges the political and social establishment through not only the historical plots she imagines but also the techniques she employs to communicate them. By drawing frequently upon a dynamic oral tradition that has preserved alternative histories, she incorporates a discourse that has not participated in the trappings of power but rather articulated resistance. An analysis of her texts reveals a preference for certain kinds of discourse, especially personal writing and reported speech (testimonials), neither of which has traditionally been privileged by either national or literary authorities. In incorporating different discourses into her novels, she creates decentralized stories that multiply interpretive possibilities. Though the stories uniformly sympathize with leftist struggles, the introduction of gender concerns, as well as the incorporation of numerous voices within a single text, highlights the contested nature of representations of both identity and history.

As Alegría creates literary space for El Salvador's polyphony, she recovers voices of protest squelched by a succession of authoritarian governments. Since independence, these regimes have insisted on a uniform national identity dependent on the stripping of both women and indigenous peoples of opportunities for self-expression.[2] By incorporating expressions of frustrations and rebellion into her texts, Alegría interrogates the accepted interpretations of history that have justified and reinforced inequities in terms of class, gender, and ethnicity.

Contextualizations: Reading Claribel Alegría in Central America

Alegría's innovative strategies of composition contributed to a new kind of writing in Central America that introduced women's voices into the cultural canon even as it reconfigured the novel. Through the efforts of writers like Alegría, Central American fiction emerged from the social realism that dominated literature prior to the 1960s. Alegría's writing in particular incorporates experimental techniques in an effort to engage the troubling social reality of the isthmus. Her success with *Cenizas de Izalco* was unprecedented for a woman author, and Alegría saw her first narrative endeavor published not only abroad but also eventually in El Salvador (Saporta Sternbach, 61).[3] This was a significant achievement not just because Alegría's text was critical of government repression but also because women's stories had only sporadically been published in Latin America. As Nancy Saporta Sternbach notes, "In 1964 it was revolutionary enough just to write about the Matanza, but to claim that women count enough so that their stories really are the stories of their countries allows us to examine women's roles in the formation of national states" (63). Alegría's dual preoccupation with women's issues and political justice creates an alternative national history that counters versions of the past long mobilized to force national solidarity and justify blatant social injustices.

Though she is not the first woman to articulate women's concerns in Central America, Claribel Alegría is the first female novelist whose prose has received extensive popular distribution and critical acclaim in Central America and abroad. She is also the author of numerous books of poetry, as well as novellas and short stories. No matter the genre, however, Alegría communicates an active concern with women as subjects. Her poetry, for example, chronicles passion, frustration, and grief using female voices. Critical recognition began with her first novel, *Cenizas de Izalco* (1966), which was a finalist in Editorial Seix Barral's Biblioteca Breve competition in 1964. The preoccupation with women as subjects in the drama of Central America is particularly prevalent in her historical novels. Each of these is intimately linked to both the revolutionary struggles of the twentieth century and the liberation of women from gender-based oppression.

In her narratives, Alegría elaborates at length a fictionalized history of El Salvador in order to bring to the foreground not only pressing social concerns but also the sexual, political, and literary awakenings of women. My analysis centers upon the reading of three texts that have an overtly historical intent: *Cenizas de Izalco, No me agarran viva* (1985), and *Despierta, mi bien, despierta* (1986). In each of these stories, the bourgeois female protagonists gradually come to criticize the established political ideology of the nation and the family that limits their human potential. The texts probe the implications of this coming to consciousness for both individual women and their communities. The stories especially emphasize the latent violence implicit in the social order, a violence that becomes explicit and overt in the face of resistance to it. In analyzing these novels, I consider the way in which Alegría imagines female resistance and recovers memory, as well as the strategies she uses to plot alternative histories in her texts. I rely particularly upon the commentary of feminist theorists of women's writing, as well upon the concepts about history and narrative posited by Hayden White.[4]

Of special interest to me in this chapter are the figures of women reading and writing that appear consistently in Alegría's fictions in association with the struggle for memory, identity, and self-expression.

In each of her overtly historical novels, Alegría presents the story of "remembering" women who become active as readers, guerrillas, and writers. The task of re-membering, or restoring what has been fragmented, is accomplished in different ways in each of the novels. The recovery of memory may occur at the story level, as in the case of *Cenizas de Izalco,* or at the textual level, as in *No me agarran viva.* The latter is itself a project of re-membering a woman fallen in combat. Though the texts are quite different, each points to the need to recuperate the past for women and others who have been marginalized.

Because of her efforts to remember the marginalized and document struggles for national liberation, Alegría has drawn more critical attention than most other Central American writers. In fact, Sandra Boschetto-Sandoval and Marcia Phillips McGowan gathered several critical essays into a book, the publication of which by a university press is testimony in itself of Alegría's ability to command an audience. Of all her writing, Alegría's novels in particular have interested many critics, among them Linda Craft, Rose Marie Galindo, Cheryl Horton Reiss, Ileana Rodríguez, Nancy Saporta Sternbach, Maureen Shea, and Mary Jane Treacy. The dialogue initiated by these authors informs my work; like each of them, I too am interested in feminist issues and Alegría's contribution to a growing body of literature that articulates these concerns in Central America. In particular, Shea's assertion that Alegría is significant in articulating a "growing awareness of sexual oppression" made me realize that this same awareness surfaces in the writing of many Central American women writers and in all those included in this study.[5]

Alegría's texts are interesting because of the way in which she integrates the stories of women's awakenings to oppression (sexual and otherwise) with fictionalized elaborations of history. The narrative works discussed in this chapter all feature plots about crucial moments of Salvadoran history during the twentieth century, including some of the most violent instances of political and social unrest. *Cenizas de Izalco* depicts the 1932 popular uprising and peasant massacre known as la Matanza, linking memories of this revolt to life in Santa Ana in the 1960s, while *No me agarran viva* and *Despierta, mi bien, despierta* concern the guerrilla struggles of the 1980s.[6] Each plot follows the trajectory of concientización; at least on a superficial level, they are narratives of progress featuring protagonists that become aware of oppression and subsequently commit themselves to personal and national liberation.

To a certain degree, Alegría's fictions are also imbricated in Marxist discourse. They consistently show the injustice inherent in capitalistic expansion and affirm the emancipatory potential of communities committed to struggles against this system. The Marxist influence has important implications for the readings these novels offer of El Salvador's present and past. As Lowe and Lloyd point out, Western Marxism shares with liberalism "a foundation in what Walter Benjamin refers to as 'historicism,' that is, the conception of history as the narrative of the development of modern subjects and cultures" (3). This conception is prevalent in the discourse of revolutionary movements in Central America and can be identified in the novels of concientización, which trace the development of subjects within a revolutionary culture.[7] However, Central American movements and texts adapt Western Marxist discourse to the peculiarities of the isthmus, hence the emphasis on campesino-worker[8] alliances and the allusions to resistance rooted in the indigenous past in many texts.

The preoccupation with female subjects in Alegría's work introduces another element into the discussion of struggle and liberation. *No me agarran viva* in particular posits a Marxist interpretation of Central American reality, yet a feminist perspective also insistently pervades this novel. This reconfigures the "narrative of development" in terms of both class and gender.

The introduction of women's concerns in the leftist writing that gained currency in the 1960s and 1970s is significant for the precedent it set for literary endeavors inside and outside the framework of revolutionary ideology. If Alegría's writing initiated the interrogation of women's positions within the context of Marxist ideology in Central America, subsequent writing by women took the challenge even further, particularly in historical fictions. For instance, Belli in *La mujer habitada* signals the fractures in the development of a new, leftist national culture. In *Sofía de los presagios* and *Waslala* she moves completely beyond the Marxist framework while still conserving an interest in women's issues.

Women, Nation, and Emancipation: History and Fiction

In El Salvador, as in other Latin American countries, there has been a continuity of oppression of working classes, traditionally comprised of *obreros* and campesinos. Alegría dramatizes the oppression of these marginalized people in her novels, and at the same time she depicts bourgeois women in their unique position as both the fellow marginalized and the socially privileged. Alegría's novels *Cenizas* and *Despierta* each feature women who suffer as a result of patriarchal prejudices and yet who ignore (for a time) their own subjugation because they have internalized the justificatory rhetoric of the male authorities in their lives. *Cenizas* makes clear the persistence of gender inequities from the 1930s to the 1960s; *Despierta's* protagonist finds herself in a similarly circumscribed world in the 1980s. Alegría's insistent representation of women's limited options underscores the fundamental problem of inequality. It also shows the repetition of the same family structures over generations. Furthermore, Alegría reveals small-town gossip and hierarchies within families as vehicles of oppression. She thus not only uncovers insidious forms of social control, she also links them to more dramatic enforcements of the status quo in the nation.

Repression in twentieth-century Latin America has roots that run through several centuries of justification, coercion, and violence as an ultimate recourse. Women's conduct was regulated first by the Church under colonial rule and then, after independence, by the newly formed states. According to Lowe and Lloyd, though other groups attained various degrees of liberation, the limitations placed upon women persisted even into the modern era: "While the modern state has in theory offered women emancipation in the economic and political spheres, and even participation in anticolonial nationalist struggles, the regulation and consolidation of national identity has generally led to women's political/juridical exclusion, their educational subordination, economic exploitation, and ideological suppression" (17). In Latin America, women's sexuality was a fundamental concern for ecclesiastical and state authorities, who sought to regulate their potentially destructive power of reproduction. Women's bodies represented a threat to the moral, political, and social stability of patriarchies interested in protecting familial prestige, racial purity, and the privilege of the few. Unlike that of men, women's sexual rebellion against established mores was not an act of personal defiance but rather was a challenge to the entire ecclesiastical or secular system (or both). Indeed, the stability of the social order was predicated upon women's compliance. Any aberration threatened the collapse of the entire structure of class distinctions based on racial or ethnic justifications.

Though seemingly incongruous with "modern" understandings of race, ethnicity, and sexuality, vestiges of these regulations remain deeply imbedded in familial and social structures. Alegría's historical fictions emphasize the forms such restrictions take in the lives of individual women. In fact, her novels chronicle a defiance of sexual mores, as well as other political challenges to the status quo, as they plot events of El Salvador's past according to an alternative ideology. Particularly in *Cenizas de Izalco* and *Despierta*, Alegría intertwines the two types of rebellion—political and sexual—to reveal the challenges posed by patriarchy's Others. In imagining specific instances of the sort of rebellion that became widespread in Central America, she also draws attention to brutal means by which those in power protected their authority. A more overtly political text, *No me agarran viva* differs slightly from the other two novels, though it does combine gender and political concerns as it recovers the memory of a fallen *guerrillera* (female combatant). As such, it creates a new sort of hero through the celebration of a woman liberated in terms of both gender and political roles.

Re-Membering the Past in Cenizas de Izalco

Cenizas de Izalco is Alegría's first novel and arguably her best narrative work. A polyphonic text that includes narration in first person, diary excerpts, analepsis and prolepsis, the novel is structurally complex and invites critical engagement on the part of the reader. The process of composition of *Cenizas* was also unusual, involving the collaboration of Alegría and her husband Darwin Flakoll.

There has generally been a collective critical silence about the role of "Bud" Flakoll, but he played a very important role in Alegría's life and literary career. In a 1996 interview in *Cultura,* Claribel Alegría spoke publicly at length for the first time about the conception of *Cenizas.* According to Alegría, she and Flakoll were living in Paris shortly after the triumph of the Cuban Revolution, an event intimately linked to the birth of her novel. The interview is the most elaborate response she has given to questions of coauthorship:

> Estábamos en París, y a mí los acontecimientos de Cuba me abrieron puertas en la conciencia. . . . Entonces se me aflojaron los recuerdos de mi infancia. Y comencé a hablar casi de manera obsesiva de mis recuerdos del 32. . . . Nunca olvidaré que fue Carlos Fuentes quien me dijo: "Claribel, tienes que escribir ésto." Le respondí que no, porque consideraba que no tenía oficio de narradora. . . . Allí saltó Bud, quien tenía mucho oficio como periodista, y me dijo: "Bueno, por qué no lo escribimos los dos." . . . Hicimos un plan. Saqué todos mis recuerdos de infancia. Entonces urdimos la historia de amor. Al principio el acuerdo fue que yo escribiría de la novela lo que correspondía al

personaje femenino, y Bud lo del personaje del gringo . . . Pero él escribía en inglés y yo se lo traducía al español . . . Uno agregaba y la otra cortaba, y allí venían los pleitos . . . Hasta que al final dijimos: vamos a trabajar juntos por el hijo, que era la novella . . . Y entonces, te juro, una vez el libro estuvo terminado, nos asombrábamos y nos preguntábamos el uno al otro, ¿quién escribió esta parte? ("Buena estrella," 91–92) [We were in Paris, and the events in Cuba opened the eyes of my conscience. . . . And then memories of my childhood began to come to me. And I began to talk almost obsessively about my memories of '32. I will never forget that it was Carlos Fuentes who told me: "Claribel, you have to write this." And then Bud, with his vocation as a journalist, jumped in and told me: "Well, why don't the two of us write it." We made a plan. I drew on all my memories of childhood. Then we wrote the love story. In the beginning, the agreement was that I would write the parts that related to the female character, and Bud, those of the gringo. But he wrote in English, and I would translate it into Spanish. . . . One would add and the other take out, and then the arguments began. . . . So we finally decided: we're going to work together for this child that is the novel. . . . And then, I swear, once the book was finished, we were shocked and asked each other, Who wrote this part?]

Though it is obvious from this explanation that Flakoll had an intimate role in the composition of the novel, the literary community has tended to overlook the collaborative effort, associating the novel with Alegría alone. This is perhaps because Salvadoran and women's issues predominate in the novel, leading readers to attribute, erroneously, the work to Alegría. For convenience, I stylistically follow suit and refer to Alegría as author throughout the discussion of *Cenizas*. By referencing Flakoll's participation, however, I hope to dispel the notion that feminist causes are solely the domain of women. True change comes only through a collaborative enterprise fraught with the same difficulties Flakoll and Alegría faced in their writing of the novel.

The plot of *Cenizas de Izalco* revolves around Carmen, a woman who returns to El Salvador from the United States. She arrives just after her ill mother has died. Carmen receives a wrapped diary that her mother Isabel bequeathed to her, and the plot unfolds as Carmen reads the diary. Saporta Sternbach suggests that "the reading of this diary . . . serves as the structural axis of the novel, since the reading itself is what triggers the unveiling, unknotting, recuperation, and recovery of her mother's story and her country's story" (63). Reading mediates the protagonist's confrontation of the past and leads her to question her identity and place in the present. As such, it becomes a vehicle for personal awakening. Indeed, throughout Alegría's work the act of reading and telling stories consistently appears as an agent of personal transformation and social change.

Interestingly enough, the diary Carmen reads belonged not to Isabel but to Frank Wolff, the American man with whom her mother had a brief affair. Thus, the image Carmen pieces together of her mother is one that has always already been "read" or filtered by another. As Alegría brings the processes of reading, interpreting, and responding to texts into focus, she also dramatizes the problems confronted by women who must recover their history in texts that feature them as objects rather than subjects of history and desire. The presentation of this process through the figure of Carmen problematizes notions of memory and identity. Carmen encounters a troubled past that had been covered with a veneer of normalcy, and she begins to formulate her own questions of identity and purpose.

Alegría gives literary representation to a process of awakening that accompanies the recovery of memory. As Carmen undertakes the reading of the diary, she begins a process of re-membering, of pulling together disparate stories in order to recover the past. She perceives this as a process intimately related to her own struggles with identity and self-fulfillment. As she pieces together revelations from the diary with her own memories and other people's anecdotes, Carmen attempts to understand both her mother and herself. In doing so, she realizes that she knows very little about her own mother. Beyond that, she recognizes that what she had presumed to know was not in fact an entirely accurate representation, but rather a partial one based on her mother's (not wholly convincing) performance of socially expected roles.

In giving a fictional reconstruction of El Salvador's past through the life of Carmen's family, *Cenizas de Izalco* introduces in the 1960s one of the recurrent themes in Central American women's texts: the search for antecedents and the confrontation of the lack of women's history. Many historical fictions written by women in the following years dramatize the same search for these antecedents, some of whom take the form of absent mothers, as in Gioconda Belli's novels about Faguas. In other cases, the antecedents are colonial women (indigenous or Spanish), whose absence is confronted by both Rosario Aguilar and Tatiana Lobo in fictions that attempt to recover their memory.

In *Cenizas* the process of re-membering and coming to terms with identity is intimately connected to the engagement of oral and written traditions. The text Carmen confronts is Frank Wolff's diary, passages of which are quoted in *Cenizas* as Carmen reads them. For Carmen, Frank's diary is imbued with authority simply because it is a written text. Unlike oral anecdotes, it proffers a fixed, invariable representation of certain events in the life of Frank Wolff. Additionally, the diary is authoritative because it was penned by a North American man who was both a writer and also an intimate of Carmen's mother; his position and his experience locate him in a position of privilege. Significantly, Frank's voice is reminiscent of that of the anthropologist participant-observer, whose renditions of people, places, and happenings in field notes and ethnographies communicate authority precisely because of their interpretive distance. The effect of this sort of representation on the reader Carmen is first a distancing from her mother, then a demystification of Frank's textual voice.

Carmen's reaction to Wolff's diary is interesting because it reveals the processes of disbelief and confusion that culminate not only in the revision of her own memory but also her questioning of other people's recollections. In one particular passage, Carmen relates her struggle to organize her memories: "Después de leer el diario de Frank me siento desorientada, como si casi no la hubiese conocido. Tengo que ordenar mis memorias, precisar mejor sus rasgos, su carácter, rescatarla del caos" (18) [After reading Frank's diary, I feel disoriented, as if I had hardly known her. I have to sort out my memories, pinpoint her features, her character, and rescue her from chaos]. The authority of Frank's account leads Carmen to doubt her own memories, but her next reaction is telling. Rather than accepting Frank's diary as the final word on her mother's life, she seeks out other accounts, especially those of Eugenia, a relative in whom her mother confided. Eugenia's testimony corroborates Frank's accounts, while also highlighting Isabel's anguish over the affair. Furthermore, each question Carmen poses to family members about both Wolff and her mother yields a different response.

The dialogue and debate between texts within *Cenizas* is particularly significant because it reveals history and identity to be constructions that are contested by various people and groups. This discursive competition in Alegría's texts attracted the attention of Cheryl Horton Reiss, who has found "an intricate web of power relations" connecting oral and written discourse in *Despierta, mi bien, despierta,* a novel in which the different modes of discourse are manipulated and controlled by different characters (133). In *Cenizas,* discourses are juxtaposed, complementing and contradicting one another, insinuating that Isabel's identity was one she negotiated and performed throughout her life. More than that, since it makes clear that different family members read Isabel's life according to their own desires and preconceived notions, the novel emphasizes the multiplication of interpretive possibilities and the constructed nature of history.

Within the story itself, the evocation of Paris by various individuals dramatizes the possibility of multiple interpretations of any given object (person or place). Carmen observes of her childhood:

"Hasta mucho tiempo después me di cuenta de que no hay un solo París" (22) [Only much later did I realize that there is not just one Paris]. Paris is a different place for Frank, her mother, father, and grandfather, and the manner in which each individual characterizes Paris reveals differences among them. Not only that, their renderings of Paris indicate what was desired by and accessible to each one of them. For instance, the Paris of Carmen's grandfather centered about the Sorbonne medical school, and her father's around the Eiffel Tower. In contrast, her mother's Paris was "[u]n París de sombras que giran alrededor del Palais Royal o están encerradas en el Panteón" (24) [a Paris of shadows that float around the Palais Royal or that are locked within the Pantheon]. A literary Paris, it was populated by "Robespierre, María Antonieta, Victor Hugo, Balzac, Lamartine" (23). Accessible to her only in books, the Paris of Isabel was the place upon which she inscribed her frustrations and her desires for escape.

While Paris for Carmen's father and grandfather (Papá Manuel) was the scene of the intellectual and sexual exploits of their youth, for her mother Paris was only accessible in textual form. Carmen reflects that "Frank se lanzó a la aventura; Papá Manuel, papá. Mamá, en cambio, nunca lo hizo. Murió viendo París a través de los recuerdos de mi abuelo, de papá, de Frank" (63) [Frank set off for adventure; Papá Manuel, Papá. Mamá, on the other hand, never did. She died seeing Paris through the memories of my grandfather, of father, of Frank]. Carmen realizes that Isabel's dreams were always brokered by others, and the Paris she lived vicariously is the symbol of these stymied desires.

Carmen remembers most vividly her mother's absorption in books in the evenings and Isabel's excitement with the preparations for infrequent trips to visit relatives: "Las memorias más nítidas que tengo de ella son mientras hace preparativos para escaparse: visitas a San Salvador donde Lola o donde Maruca, escasos viajes a Guatemala o México. . . . No esconde su alegría" (19) [The sharpest memories I have are of her as she made her preparations to escape: visits to San

Salvador, to Lola's or Maruca's, rare trips to Guatemala or Mexico. . . . She couldn't hide her joy]. Alegría emphasizes throughout the novel that the same imperative for escape persists in Isabel's daughter, Carmen, even though Carmen's circumstances are superficially very different. While Isabel thinks life would be better if she could just leave Santa Ana, her daughter suffers the same frustration, even though she was educated abroad and lives in Washington, D.C.

In drawing the parallel between mother and daughter so insistently, Alegría suggests that there is a deeper structural reason for their sense of confinement. As Shea has noted, the alienation Carmen and Isabel experience stems not from their lives in a certain time or place but rather from roles imposed upon them by patriarchal society (64). For both women, their marital relationships are the principal instruments of their containment as individuals, enforcing the roles that so stifle them. Neither Carmen nor her mother enjoys a union that would allow them to be themselves. Of her mother, Carmen notes, "Recordándola me da la sensación de alguien que llevaba un bulto muy pesado y sólo se libraba de él cuando estaba fuera de casa o escondida entre sus libros. Ese peso no pudo haber sido otro que papá" (19–20) [Remembering her gives me the impression of someone carrying a heavy load from which she is free only when she was out of the house or buried in her books. That weight could not have been anyone but Papá]. Carmen's own relationship with her husband Paul leaves much to be desired, according to various hints she gives in the text: "Paul es buen marido si con eso se quiere decir un buen proveedor. Me llena de máquinas, de aire acondicionado, de aparatos de televisión. . . . Nunca discute mis reproducciones de abstractos. . . . Le habría convenido otra mujer; conmigo no se siente cómodo" (83) [Paul is a good husband if by that you mean a good provider. He loads me down with appliances, with air conditioners, with televisions. He never discusses my reproductions of abstracts. . . . Some other woman would have suited him; with me he doesn't feel comfortable]. Numerous passages allude to Carmen's unhappiness and isolation, products of a familial and community structure that gives women little space for expression. In fact, Alegría suggests that the situation might be worse for Carmen as an immigrant living in the suburbs, without a community of women to share her frustrations. The emphasis on women's sense of futility, as well as their need for escape, is a theme that Alegría dramatizes forcefully in *Cenizas*. It also resurfaces in her later novel *Despierta, mi bien, despierta*. In portraying women's frustration in conjunction with thwarted attempts at political resistance, Alegría points a finger at the inequality inherent in Salvadoran society, a patriarchal culture that depends on the subjugation of the majority to secure the privilege and pleasure of the few. The same combination of themes occurs in the texts of other Central American women writers, perhaps most insistently in the novels of Rosario Aguilar (see chapter 3).

Throughout the novel, Alegría shows that both the reading of the diary and the imagination of the turbulent past it reconstructs, prompt Carmen to self-reflection. The reading fosters in Carmen a developing awareness about herself and the life she leads more than three decades after her mother's affair and the massacre of 1932. *Cenizas* makes clear that the same inequalities persist without resolution and that the protagonist becomes aware of them only by engaging the past and deciphering its implications for her own existence.

Because of this preoccupation with the recovery and interpretation of the past, it is possible to read *Cenizas* as a metafictional text about the act of reading, about a woman's act of combing texts (mostly male-authored) in search of an understanding of herself and her past. As one of the first overtly historical novels by a Central American woman, *Cenizas* is particularly interesting in that it links an individual's coming to consciousness with active confrontation of the past and the truth claims of accepted representations of events. It is also significant that a female figure is employed to critique "established political ideologies," as Higonnet puts it ("Civil Wars," 80–81). The innovative polyphonic narrative that tells her story dramatizes the challenge posed by women to the traditions that have ensured or enforced their complicity with the status quo.

In *Cenizas* there is a protagonist who, when confronted with the absence of her mother's voice (and diary), reads between the self-absorbed lines of another's diary in an attempt to understand her own history. As Carmen begins to read, the male-authored text threatens to become the authoritative version of her mother and to subsume all of Carmen's own memories into its emplotment. The diary troubles Carmen's evaluation of past events. For example, it prompts Carmen to reconsider Isabel's reactions to certain circumstances, such as Isabel's obvious discomfort at her husband's laughter in camaraderie with other men. However, Frank's novel ultimately does not assume the place of authority; rather, in reaction Carmen seeks out alternative testimonies, those expressed to her orally by other family members. Through this process, Carmen is eventually able to recognize the limitations of her own idealizations of her mother, as well as the constructedness of Frank's vision of the world. In short, she becomes a reader and critic of texts. In patching together a narrative of voices and understanding the dialogue among them, she sheds light not only on her own family history but also on that of the Salvadoran nation.

Significantly, in *Cenizas* Alegría constructs the text in such a way that the reader accompanies Carmen in her reading. The text signals the reader to "fill in the gaps of the text" (to use Wolfgang Iser's phrase) alongside the protagonist.[9] This is evident in the structure of the text, in which passages from the diary appear and conclude without any introduction. The overall effect is a confusion of past and present, and the blurring of the distinction between them emphasizes the fluidity of the passage of time and the persistence of common structures in different epochs. For instance, as Carmen processes the surprising information she gleans about her own past, the text increasingly confronts the reader with an alternative history of both that family in particular and the Salvadoran people as a whole. This technique brings the 1932 peasant uprising to the forefront in the last pages of the novel, since Frank gives a dramatic account of the rebellion and its brutal suppression. The use of the diary to introduce the 1932 massacre not only permits the elaboration of details about past events but also creates a sense of suspense that would otherwise have been impossible to construe. After all, the results of the Matanza are clearly visible in the textual present.

After relating the violent climax of events in 1932, the novel returns rather abruptly to the primary narrative in Carmen's voice, in which she remembers her mother's burial: "Con una pala le siguieron echando tierra, tierra negra del volcán. . . . Sigue cayendo la tierra, cubriéndola, cubriéndolos a todos" (209) [With a shovel, they kept throwing earth on her, black earth from the volcano. . . . The earth keeps falling, covering her, covering them all]. The allusion to "tierra del volcán," as well as the use of the present progressive tense with a plural object, intimates that neither the repression nor the resistance to it is gone. Rather, they lie beneath the surface, to erupt again in the next generation.

The conclusion signals anew the preoccupation with the present that pervades the novel. In the case of *Cenizas*, the story of a woman who begins to question her past, read, and collect oral testimony in order to come to terms with her own problems is extremely suggestive of the revolutionary process in El Salvador. Especially in the 1960s, when the novel was published, leftist groups began to seize upon the legacy of Farabundo Martí and so posit alternative imaginations of the national past.[10] They began to question the way in which these events had been plotted, and with their questioning they revealed the ideological contingency of the historical record that had been mobilized to support a national identity. Though *Cenizas* seems at first to focus primarily on one woman's search for her mother, both the conclusion and the frequent allusions to the political and social reality make clear the broader, national preoccupations Alegría had in the composition of the novel. In her imagination of the past, Alegría emphasizes that not only has little changed in terms of options for women (Carmen is still frustrated and isolated even in the capital of the capitalist world), little has changed politically in El Salvador since the uprising.

For this reason, the last pages (which function almost as a postscript), are highly significant for the interpretation of the text. In her comments about the tierra del volcán and the discovery of "*otro rostro*" (another face), Alegría suggests the persistence of latent resistance as well as alternative histories. Certainly the racial and ethnic prejudices persist; Alegría reveals these throughout the text, mostly in the speech of relatives and mourners who come to give their condolences to Carmen. However, beneath the surface of normalcy there is evidence of discontent, recorded mostly in popular traditions and the oral culture. These represent another "rostro" of the nation that can be recovered through a re-membering of the past. As Carmen recovers the memory of her mother, so too, Alegría suggests, the Salvadoran people may re-member their own troubled past and act to remedy their present straits.

Women in Revolution: Reconstructing Lives in No me agarran viva

Like *Cenizas de Izalco,* the testimonial "novel" *No me agarran viva* is also a text concerned about the recuperation of the past, in this case, the legacy of a guerrillera who died in the struggle for national liberation in the early 1980s. The intent of *No me agarran* is more overtly political than in *Cenizas.* In fact, Mary Jane Treacy has suggested the novel undertakes the construction of the "woman warrior," a new heroic model born of the Central American revolutionary movements (75–76). In my analysis, I am concerned not so much with the image of the guerrillera as with the techniques Alegría employs in the creation of a woman's "biography" of a radically different sort.

No me agarran viva is a text at once biographical and testimonial. Like *Cenizas,* it was written with the active collaboration of Darwin Flakoll. On his role, Alegría explains that "los testimonios los hicimos Bud y yo, juntos; y Bud es el piloto" ("Buena estrella," 92) [Bud and I wrote the testimonies together; and Bud is the pilot]. The innovative strategies Alegría and Flakoll employed in its construction demonstrate their continued concern for the recuperation of women's voices and, ultimately, the history of women as it relates to the life of the nation. The full title, *No me agarran viva: La mujer salvadoreña en lucha* suggests this, though the plot revolves around the life of a single woman, Eugenia, a young Salvadoran guerrillera. Nevertheless, while *No me agarran* is very much about Eugenia's life and death, it is also about the recuperation of alternative histories and the problems and possibilities of their representation in literature.

The representation of "la mujer salvadoreña en lucha" [the Salvadoran woman in the struggle] in *No me agarran* is accomplished through a manipulation of genres and discourses. The hybrid nature of the text has made the classification of the book problematic for critics. Combining techniques of the novel, documentary fiction, testimonial narrative, and journalistic writing, it is a text that challenges traditional distinctions between fact and fiction. Ten chapters comprise the book; they carry no titles, only numbers, and are organized around certain thematic concerns: induction into revolutionary activity, married life, machismo, children, and so on. Each chapter is introduced by a fictionalized passage that presents a context to frame subsequent narrative (ch. 1), a brief presentation of the individual to whom Alegría and Flakoll posed their questions (ch. 3), or a short "topic sentence" (ch. 4). The memories of Eugenia's friends and family, indicated in the text with quotation marks, comprise the majority of each chapter and together form a chorus of voices that reconstruct her life and person.

This unique composition has a great deal in common with ethnographic texts; it employs many of the same strategies of elicitation and composition utilized by anthropologists. It shares much with postmodern ethnography, such as that described by George Marcus, who points out that Immanuel Wallerstein's "world system perspective," introduced in the 1970s, provided "a framework for the intimate reassociation of history and social theory" that made ethnography "sensitive to its context of historical political economy" (167). This same insistence upon contextualization permeates the pages of *No me agarran*, which includes passages documenting national, regional, and world issues; these frequently appear between extended portions of reported speech. Like ethnographers during the same period, Alegría and Flakoll carefully situate their story about Eugenia within a narrative of a larger scope. This is immediately evident in the prologue, in which the authors state that Eugenia "es un caso típico y no excepcional de tantas mujeres salvadoreñas" (9) [is a typical, not an exceptional, example of so many Salvadoran women]; her story is representative of many others. Furthermore, events are located within the context of not only the Salvadoran revolutionary struggle but also regional developments such as the Sandinista victory in Nicaragua, as well as the overarching global reality of Cold War hostilities.

For the authors as for the Salvadoran combatants they quote, Marxism offers a ready interpretive paradigm for integrating accounts of local struggles within a comprehensive theory of history and society. Though Marxist conceptualizations do inform *No me agarran*, the text is neither a political treatise nor a work of social realism. Through unusual strategies of composition, Alegría and Flakoll avoid the adoption of an authoritative voice and limit the order they impose on the re-membering of Eugenia's life. Most important, they retain the dialogic nature of the text's construction. Some passages are summaries of events, but even these often contain long quotes interjected to validate the narrative.

In places, the authors also make transparent the processes of elicitation they employed. In doing so, they make themselves visible by recording some of their questions and interspersing the pronoun *we* at periodic intervals. Consider, for example, this passage from chapter 6: "¿Qué efectos psicológicos y políticos tuvo el triunfo de la revolución sandinista sobre el movimiento revolucionario de El Salvador?—le preguntamos a Javier" (87–88) [What psychological and political effects did the triumph of the Sandinista revolution have on the revolutionary movement of El Salvador?—we asked Javier]. In a subsequent chapter, they ask, "¿Qué nos pueden decir sobre la participación de los niños en las tareas revolucionarias?" (99) [What can you tell us about the participation of children in revolutionary activities?]. These questions serve to contextualize the story and transition between topics. They also indicate to the reader the presence of interviewees who control (to some extent) the dialogue. This distinguishes *No me agarran* from some other mediated testimonials, most notably that of Rigoberta Menchú, in which editor Elizabeth Burgos-Debray effectively erased herself from the text and subsequently refused to disclose her questions. In contrast, *No me agarran* does confront the reader with the presence of an interlocutor located outside the events described in the text, signaling again the constructedness of the history it tells.

From its inception, *No me agarran* not only reveals an overtly historical intent, but also blurs the boundaries between various genres of narrative. In fact, the entire text troubles the border between documentary and fiction, journalism and the novel. In doing so, it emphasizes again the constructedness of all these representations. The narrative is cinematographic in many instances, and like a documentary film, it includes interviews, description, and brief recantations of historical events. Furthermore, it offers multiple interpretations of the identity of the woman Eugenia, including commentary by those who knew her as a student, daughter, revolutionary, wife, mother, and leader. While reconstructing the life of a single individual, Alegría and Flakoll emphasize that Eugenia's story is the same as that of hundreds of women who have fallen and will not be forgotten.

Despite the obviously testimonial gestures, *No me agarran* differs from other testimonials in a number of ways. First, though it tells the story of an individual representative of a collective, it does not contain her voice. The subject of *No me agarran* is Eugenia, a woman who has already died and thus can no longer speak for herself; the only portions of the text narrated in her voice are two letters that are reproduced in the final pages of the text. In addition, the text is organizationally complex, unlike the fairly straightforward first-person narratives of other testimonials from Latin America. Though the chapters of *No me agarran* adhere to a certain chronological progression culminating in the death of Eugenia, the incorporation of multiple voices and memories means that the text moves back and forth in time around any given theme. Thus, the text constantly challenges the reader to revise her understanding of the protagonist Eugenia and the other Salvadoran women of whom she is representative.

The first pages reconstruct the "action" in which Eugenia died, presenting the scene like an action sequence from a movie or novel. Indeed, the first paragraph begins dramatically: "Eugenia se tumbó de bruces en el suelo, inspeccionó el lote de armas escondido debajo del vehículo y verificó que cada una de ellas estaba bien envuelta en trapos que las protegían del polvo" (11) [Eugenia fell flat on the ground and inspected the cache of arms under the vehicle, and she made sure that each one was well wrapped in rags to protect it from the dust]. The rapid-fire succession of active verbs creates a fast-moving sequence of events, and the mention of hidden arms immediately introduces an element of danger. The first few paragraphs also carefully specify the historical context, locate the actions in time and space, and reference them in terms of the international debate about communism, revolution, and national sovereignty. After the first novelistic chapter, the format changes to one that dominates the remainder of the book. Here named individuals appear to relate anecdotes and complete a picture of Eugenia, who can no longer speak for herself. The effort of re-membering, like that of revolution, is a collective one.

Through the memories of others, authors Alegría and Flakoll recuperate the human face of civil uprising. Both the narrative technique and explicit contestation challenge the representation of El
Salvador elaborated by Cold War rhetoric in currency in the 1980s.
At a time in which the revolutionary movements in both Nicaragua
and El Salvador were the targets of Reagan's vituperation, *No me
agarran* posits an alternative emplotment of events in the region. Important in this is the inclusion of individuals with names, personal
histories, and memories, all of which counter the sweeping general-
izations of Cold War discourse. Significantly, the individuals included in the text are presented in terms not only of their position
within the revolutionary organization but also of their relationships
with one another as friends and family. This revelation of specific
individuals behind the abstractions of the media is a powerful counter-
discourse. In some cases, Alegría responds overtly to the representations of the conflict made by the U.S. government. The engagement
of right-wing political discourse is explicit in the chapter dedicated to
Marina González. After briefly introducing Marina, "una arquetípica
mujer proletaria de El Salvador" [an archetypical proletarian woman
from El Salvador], the authors wryly suggest that if "el presidente
Reagan y sus consejeros realmente quisieran saber por qué el pueblo
salvadoreño está en pie de lucha, aprenderían mucho más escuchando
la vida de Marina González que buscando pruebas de hipotéticos
complots cubanos o soviéticos" (110) [President Reagan and his advisers would really like to know why the Salvadoran people are fighting, they would learn much more by listening to the life of Marina
González than by looking for proof of hypothetical Cuban or Soviet
conspiracies]. Though there are only a few such overt allusions, it is
clear that the text participates actively in the debate about Central
America's past and present.

Despite its obvious engagement of a political debate, *No me agarran viva* is not just a leftist text dedicated to raising consciousness
and building solidarity. It is a manual about the recuperation of alter-

native histories, in this case concerning women's involvement in the struggle for Salvadoran national liberation. The book reveals one strategy for imagining and presenting an alternative history. A unique composition that respects the voices of others, the text presents stories that are "necessarily fragmented" (Gramsci's phrase, 54) in an innovative way. The resulting literary collage is one that pieces together the particular life of Eugenia and that of el pueblo for which she stands. Like a collage, it presents a whole image yet reveals the seams in its composition. In the case of *No me agarran viva,* the presence of the seams reinforces its message about a country torn apart, only able to be recovered when many may express their voices.

Sexual and Political Awakenings in
Despierta, mi bien, despierta

Like *No me agarran, Despierta, mi bien, despierta* also concerns the realities of civil war. More than any other of Alegría's historical texts, however, *Despierta, mi bien, despierta,* presents the image of a patriarchy in crisis. According to Alegría's interpretation in this novel, the crisis that convulses both family and nation is a result of the frustrated attempts of the patriarchy—in this case, Salvadoran, bourgeois, and conservative—to persuade and intimidate the majority upon whose subjugation the stability of the state depends.

Sharing much in common with her earlier *Album familiar* (1982), variously classified as novella and short story, *Despierta* follows one woman's transformation from complicity with to rejection of the social order. *Despierta* differs, though, in both narrative sophistication and plot development. Where *Album familiar* stops at the moment of *compromiso* (commitment), *Despierta* proceeds beyond that moment to catalogue the brutality with which resistance was met. It also contains metaliterary commentary on the importance of women's writing. The novel might easily be classified as a novel of concientización, almost a subgenre by this point in Central American literature, so standard did its form become. The process of concientización that Alegría depicts in *Despierta*, however, involves the act of writing, a principal instrument in the protagonist's awakening.

As the protagonist, Lorena, changes from passivity to subjectivity, she begins to express herself in both her diary and a novel she drafts. Formerly the site upon which other people (namely her husband and the state) inscribed their own desires, her body gradually becomes eroticized and politicized. Lorena becomes a desiring, acting person, and for this reason she is dangerous. When confronted with the threat that her awakened self represents, her husband reacts with violence. Lorena competes for power he once enjoyed exclusively; she threatens the supremacy of male authority over *his* wife, *his* country, *his* ordering of the world.

A symbol of el pueblo and of women who begin to realize their power, the protagonist gradually achieves an understanding of her own subjugation and potential. Through this female figure, Alegría mounts a critique of authoritarian rule at the same time that she interjects the idea of the authoring of texts into the narrative of concientización. It is especially significant that the female protagonist's awakening is coupled with her writing of a fictionalized autobiography. Her act of writing represents a particular appropriation of history with an eye to ordering the world according to new priorities, plots, and desires.

In many ways, *Despierta* may be seen as a logical sequel to *Cenizas de Izalco*, if not in terms of characters or plot then in terms of its preoccupations with women's efforts to exercise control over their lives. In *Cenizas*, Carmen is led to question her position in society as a result of reading her mother's life, and she re-members the figure of her deceased mother through the study of Frank's diary and the collection of anecdotes from relatives. As she confronts her lack of understanding of her mother's life and identity, she questions her own existence. However, the novel never intimates that she takes any concrete action as a result, and the ending offers only minimal closure. *Despierta* picks up where *Cenizas* left off, presenting a middle-aged female protagonist bored with her comfortable life and anxious for change. Unlike Carmen, who is concerned mostly with the past, Lorena cannot ignore the urgency of the present. Additionally, she not only collects stories, she writes them and begins to order her world through the composition of fiction. *Despierta* is then not only a novel about coming to consciousness but also a metafictional text that comments on the practice of writing. Through the figure of the writing woman in *Despierta*, Alegría imagines the recent past of El Salvador, linking women's taking up of the pen to both a new awareness of reality and the possibility of a different world.

For women to take up writing in Latin America means the defiance of a cultural legacy of objectification and silence. Traditionally both women and the nation have been the objects of a discourse that affirms masculine subjectivity by creating an Other available for men to act upon at will. The Other was the site upon which male subjects inscribed their hopes, fears, and desires. For this reason, both women and the national territory have appeared in literature as indomitable and promising, dangerous yet inviting. For example, Margarita Zamora notes the gendering female of the colonial object (both territory and Indian) in Columbus's diaries.[11] Similar tendencies exist in the writings of nineteenth-century poets like Andrés Bello. His "Agricultura de la zona tórrida" begins with metaphors of love, fertility, and conception to describe the potential of the Latin American landscape. Allusions to the abundant fertility of nature abound in the literature of modernism, as does the insistence that this exuberance be dominated and channeled (by men) toward productive participation in the world economy.

It is against this legacy of male subjectivity and female passivity in terms of national identity that Alegría writes. In *Despierta* she fictionalizes the historical reality of women writing, showing her protagonist's engagement of the structures that have prevented her from acting through the medium of literature. By means of another poly-phonic narrative, *Despierta* documents the threat that the awakened woman presents to the bourgeois, nationalist system defended by people like Lorena's husband and his associates. The novel follows the radical metamorphosis of Lorena from a passive member of the social order who has internalized an authoritarian value system, into the subject of her own discourse.

Like other narratives by Central American women, the novel is a bildungsroman, in this case of a woman who appropriates words and attempts to manipulate a language and culture that had formerly classified and controlled her.[12] Lorena becomes aware of her own po-tential by acting on her desire to write. Also, through an affair with Eduardo, a member of a revolutionary organization, she experiences a sexual awakening and begins to question her lack of satisfaction with her husband and all that he represents. By means of her writing, Lorena begins to exert her will in her personal space, only to find that her actions have greater implications in terms of the nation.

By leaving her home to attend a writing workshop, Lorena sym-bolically ends her period of enclosure amid the trappings of prosper-ity that had lulled her into passivity. It is significant that her decision to take classes was opposed by her husband, Ernesto (who warned her about student subversives), and backed by her daughter, with whom Lorena feels a certain solidarity. After leaving the cloistered world of her home, Lorena enters a space where she takes on an ac-tive role in constructing the terms of her own existence. Her writing itself becomes an act of rebellion. What follows is an awakening: so-cial and psychological as a writer, sexual as Eduardo's lover, and po-litical as a sympathizer with leftist movements. Alegría's protagonist identifies writing as a key to this awakening: "Me casé profunda-mente enamorada. Lo que decía Ernesto era el credo para mí. Mi primer acto de rebeldía fue hace unos meses, al inscribirme en el taller" (49) [I married, deeply in love. What Ernesto said was law for me. My first act of rebellion was a few months ago, when I enrolled in the workshop]. Significantly, the novel emphasizes that Lorena's decision to write initiated her transformation.

Though she depicts Lorena's concientización as occurring during her affair with Eduardo, Alegría is careful not to create a fiction in which women's liberation is accounted for by the tutelage of their lovers. Instead, the female protagonist changes as the result of numerous influences, including that of her mother, her daughter, Monseñor Romero, and Eduardo. Interestingly, these are all gendered feminine in Ernesto's discourse. For example, priests are men in dresses who threaten the nation, hence his expression, "Haga patria, mate un cura" [Be patriotic, kill a priest] (17). Ultimately, though, Lorena defies even those who have supported her, opting to leave her husband, continue to write, and remain in the country. The result, of course, is a slow approximation of violence toward her person, a possibility of which she is aware and which, significantly, she identifies with gender: "Qué difícil ser mujer. Por lo menos aquí. Si obedeces acabas embruteciéndote; si empiezas a desobedecer, las consecuencias son duras" (49) [How difficult to be a woman. At least here. If you obey, you end up depraved; if you begin to disobey, the consequences are harsh]. Through such a representation, Alegría signals the underlying violence that maintains the social order.

According to the novel, women's writing poses a challenge to established social structures. As Horton Reiss points out, first Eduardo's revolutionary discourse and then Lorena's vie for supremacy in *Despierta* (134). Writing is important in the text, and women's composition is shown as a nascent discourse that competes for power. Indeed, Lorena's writing of a thinly veiled, autobiographical love story provokes a coming to consciousness and prompts a problematization of the status quo.

Alegría also emphasizes throughout that writing accompanies Lorena's political and sexual awakening. Again Horton Reiss asserts that this is significant because Lorena's incipient novel and her diary "reinforce the primacy of written discourse by focussing attention on the writing process itself" (135). She adds that the references to other texts, including newspapers and novels, "document the protagonist's development of a self-referential identity and connect the fictional world to the 'real world' context of contemporary Salvadoran society" (135). It is through this autobiographical writing, then, that Lorena begins to think for herself, explore her own desires, and effect a change in her personal life and the community.

This representation of women's autobiographical writing in a novel is significant, for autobiographical texts have attracted much attention from feminist critics in recent years. In an article on the subject, Ien Ang cites Janet Gunn's work *Autobiography* (1982) as she posits a reconceptualization of the genre: "If, as Janet Gunn has put it, autobiography is not conceived as 'the private act of a self writing' but as 'the cultural act of a self reading,' then what is at stake in autobiographical discourse is not the narcissistic representation of the subject's authentic 'me,' but the narrative construction of a subject's social location through the active interpretation of experiences that one calls one's own in particular, 'worldly' contexts" (543). This "narrative construction of a subject's social location" by a woman writing is precisely what Alegría dramatizes through the figure of Lorena in *Despierta*. However, the context of civil unrest makes the repercussions of this "cultural act of reading" dangerous in ways not commonly cited in Western feminist studies of autobiography.

As Lorena awakens politically and sexually (a process she records in her writing), she becomes a threat to the patriarchy in crisis. She begins to read herself in not only political but also erotic terms. Each proves sufficiently menacing to provoke brutal reprisals from the conservative political establishment her husband represents. In one reflection on her life, Lorena comments on her sexual experiences, then describes the change in herself in terms of an awakening: "Antes me daba rabia, me sentía usada casi no experimentaba ningún placer. Ahora con Ernesto ya ni rabia siento. . . . Veintún años en la oscuridad, la mitad de mi vida. . . . Algo me está pasando. No soy la misma

44

Lorena" (33–34) [Before it made me mad; I felt used so I didn't feel any pleasure. Now with Ernesto I don't even feel angry anymore. . . . Twenty-one years in the dark, half my life. Something is happening to me. I'm not the same Lorena]. According to Susan Rosowski, the theme of awakening occurs often in women's literature, in which "movement is inward, toward greater self-knowledge that leads in turn to a revelation of the disparity between that self-knowledge and the nature of the world" (49). This is precisely the process documented by *Despierta*, though in the context of civil war the negative reaction to female subjectivity is more overtly violent. This is certainly the case for Lorena. As she develops into a thinking, desiring person, she becomes a more serious challenge to the order Ernesto defends and thus finds herself in a position of great vulnerability.

In the novel, numerous textual clues produce a sense of the inevitability of violence. Danger approximates steadily toward the person of Lorena. Significantly, the accusations her husband and his assistant make against her are all sexual, as are the warnings she receives; these intend to convert her into an object again. For instance, Ernesto's assistant makes obscene phone calls to her, and Ernesto himself acts upon his suspicions of infidelity with violence: "En mangas de camisa y con el rostro descompuesto Ernesto irrumpió en la habitación y sin decirte nada te dio una bofetada en la mejilla con la mano abierta. 'Puta'—gruñó—, 'sos una puta'" (58) [In short sleeves and with an altered countenance, Ernesto burst into the room and without saying a word, struck you across the cheek with his open hand. Whore—he grunted—you're a whore]. In this climactic scene, Alegría makes it clear that there is no room for dialogue between equals in Ernesto's world. For him, Lorena as wife must always be subject to his desires, and her open rebellion warrants his verbal and physical abuse. Ernesto's recurrence to the most disparaging insults of his *machista* world, as well as to force, reveal the underlying violence of the system with which Lorena had cooperated up until that point. The unreasoned reaction of Ernesto thus seals the process of awakening for Lorena, determining her rejection and separation from a lifestyle that had lulled her into complicity.

The consequence of Lorena's decision is a gradual approximation of violence toward her personal space. It culminates in her discovery of Eduardo's severed head in the front seat of her beloved convertible. The novel ends abruptly after this scene, and it is significant that the motive for Eduardo's murder remains open to speculation. Neither Lorena nor the reader can ultimately know if the killing was motivated by Ernesto's political fear or his possessive jealousy.

Ultimately, the ambiguous ending intimates that women who have been awakened, either erotically or politically, are an intolerable menace to an uncompromising patriarchal culture. In the process of awakening, Lorena writes stories that rend the patriarchal façade. These gradually lead her to the realization that her life of peaceful prosperity is founded on the exploitation of others and on the suppression of her own human desires. The violent conclusion represents a last desperate attempt by those in power to wrest the word away from their challengers, and ultimately changes Lorena's autobiographical romance into a novel of concientización.

The story that Lorena both lives and writes thus becomes a metaphor for women awakening and for the nation of El Salvador. It parallels the story of the Salvadoran pueblo, which in the 1970s and 1980s began to realize its potential to write its own story. There, the brutality with which the dictatorship, the military, and their wealthy supporters reacted, pointed to the fact that the identity, progress, and prosperity of the nation had long been predicated on the sheer power of the oppressors and the complicity of many. Like Lorena, some of the silent (silenced) were "awakened" by the increasing violence.

Despierta is different from many novels like it, however, in that its fictionalization of history shows not only the process of concientización but also the role of literature in personal and national liberation. For Lorena, the process of elaborating her life in the pages of the diary and fictions leads to heightened self-awareness. It also provokes savage reprisals against her by those threatened by her nascent subjectivity. In constructing such a story, Alegría offers a metafictional commentary on the potential of writing for women. Their telling of lives becomes a vehicle not only for their own liberation but also for the transformation of the world in which they imagine themselves.

Reading the Past, Writing the Present

In *Despierta,* as in *Cenizas de Izalco* and *No me agarran viva,* Alegría fictionalizes history to reveal the unresolved tensions within the national community as it had been imagined by those in power. Her woman-centered texts also consistently challenge the nature of social relationships. They emphasize that political machinations exist in the family and the nation and that both familial and national structures have historically been predicated upon the subjugation of the Other. When this Other begins to read (Carmen), fight (Eugenia), and write (Lorena), she does not just confront the nature of her own identity; she also questions the society in which she finds herself. For all of Alegría's characters, this leads to frustration with socially sanctioned options, a questioning of accepted norms, and a new understanding of self.

The conjunction of ideas Alegría introduces recurs in other fictionalizations of history by Central American women. For instance, the novels of Gioconda Belli, the subject of the next chapter, feature women and politics (sexual and revolutionary) in the Nicaraguan context. And as with Alegría's protagonists, when these women read and write the past, foundational myths crumble and genres bend. The history of Central America becomes a space of alternative emplotments.

Chapter 2

The Quest for the Mother

Women and Memory in the Novels of Gioconda Belli

> To have a history is to possess an identity. Without memory there can
> be no personal identity in any meaningful sense of that term.
> —Siep Stuurman, "In the Long Run We Shall All Be Dead"

REBELLIOUS, INDEPENDENT, AND sexually self-assured women
populate the imagined worlds of Gioconda Belli's fictions. They are
professionals, guerrillas, and landowners; they are also mothers and
daughters. But like the woman imagined by Freud, their lack defines
them, and the novels center around the resolution of this deficiency.
Far from that lack so famously posited by Freud, however, these protagonists lack a female tradition, a memory of their mothers or female
antecedents, that will center them and enable their empowerment.

Gioconda Belli's three novels published to date, *La mujer habitada*
(1988), *Sofía de los presagios* (1992), and *Waslala* (1996), show the same
fundamental preoccupation with women's identity evidenced in the
works of Claribel Alegría. Her memoirs, published as *El país bajo mi
piel* in Spain in 2001, follow in the same vein. All of Belli's narratives
share a concern with coming of age and are stories of limitations,

rebellion, and a quest for identity and subjectivity. And despite the differences among Belli's fictions, there is one recurring narrative throughout: the confrontation of women of their lack of history and their search for empowerment through a connection with their past.

Belli's writing both reflects and challenges gender stereotypes as it engages Western and Central American narrative traditions, which have largely excluded women or imagined for them an identity and a memory that is not their own. In my analysis, I show how each novel gives a fictionalized account of women confronting history (both personal and national) as they seek a space for speaking and acting. The inversions of male national allegories and the appropriation of narrative forms, strategies, and techniques are of special concern to me because they figure prominently in Belli's woman-centered version of Central American reality.

The literary traditions Belli appropriates are intimately and inextricably linked to the nation-building process. Allen Carey-Webb notes that "literary texts participate in the making of national subjects and thus are implicated in the politics of the nation" (7). National subjects were assumed to be male, for "masculinity was established as the foundation of the nation, and women were idealized as a source of morality that simultaneously provided a background for the activity of men who determined the national fate" (24). In Latin America from the nineteenth century onward, national identities were deployed through newspapers, journals, and literary and political circles, as well as novels. This image of the individual was one largely informed by the liberal desire for progress and order, a utopian ideal frequently premised upon racism, fear of miscegenation, and the imitation of European culture. Women consistently served as metaphors, "background" for the activity of men.

In Central America, traditional national allegories eventually found their challenges in twentieth-century revolutionary programs such as the Sandinista movement, in which Belli participated. Revolutionary groups questioned unjust political and economic structures, but they still had overwhelmingly male-centered agendas. In fact, Gayatri Spivak notes that "if one considers recent historical examples, one is obliged to suggest that even if, in the crisis of armed or peaceful struggle, women seem to emerge as comrades, with the return of the everyday *and in the pores of the struggle,* the old codings of the gendered body, sometimes slightly altered, seem to fall back into place" (83; emphasis in original). As she acknowledges in her memoirs, Gioconda Belli participated in exactly the transformation Spivak describes; she went (complicitly) from militant to secretary-lover. Her three novels likewise reveal that the process of finding one's subjectivity is fraught with difficulty and necessitates an understanding of one's self and one's past.

In dialogue with earlier literature and the social text of Central America, Belli's novels suggest "other possible plots" (to use Jean Franco's phrase). They reject images of feminine passivity traditionally propagated by the Latin American (male) national imagination and vindicate a female erotic. They also reclaim a colonized memory, place women in forbidden places and roles, and suggest an alternative interpretation of Central American reality.

Belli's fiction overtly rejects stereotyped gender roles and the male allegories that posited them. Absent these models for behavior, there is a vacuum that must be filled with other "mothers" and stories. In creating female antecedents for her protagonists and woman-centered texts for the reading public, Belli supplements the story of the nation. She also appropriates the history of Nicaragua, absorbing it into a chronicle about women's search for memory, identity, and subjectivity.

Mother-Daughter Plots in Belli's Fiction: The Imperative of Memory

In her fictionalizations of history, Belli participates in a deconstructive (and reconstructive) process, challenging representations and

recovering a legacy of resistance. Her manipulation of textual traditions problematizes present world orders and promotes a different
vision of women's subjectivity. Patriarchal narratives are deeply
imbedded in cultural traditions and narrative forms. Belli appropriates one of these—the bildungsroman—and toys with it to make it
woman centered. The bildungsroman is traditionally a Western narrative type centered around the individual's search for self and integration into society; James Joyce's *A Portrait of the Artist as a Young
Man* (1916) is a quintessential example. Susan Gohlman notes the
principal components of a bildungsroman: "a young hero (usually
male), a wide range of experiences, and a sense of the ultimate practi-
cal value of these experiences later in life" (4). The bildungsroman
according to Belli is the story of a young woman confronted by a crisis in her life. In each of the stories the missing mother (a biological or
cultural antecedent) is an element crucial to the resolution of the crisis. Unlike their male predecessors, who simply must choose their
place in a patriarchal order, the protagonists in Belli's three novels
seek a past that does not exclude them and forebears with whom they
can identify in the present. Only then can they begin to construct an
identity not founded on stereotypes and become actors, rather than
the background, of history.

Each of Belli's fictional endeavors features a protagonist who attempts to negotiate her identity in a culture hostile toward her and in
which she feels herself an outsider. This sort of protagonist is common in the telling of women's stories. In fact, theorists of the genre
have noted that "female autobiographers are often motivated to write
by their awareness of the ways their identities have been constructed"
(Hite, xv). Unlike the typical male hero of the bildungsroman, the
heroine of these nineteenth-century stories cannot conform and be
integrated into society precisely because she is a woman. Seeking acceptance means the negation of her own desires and the assumption
of a socially prescribed role. Molly Hite notes, "To be marginal to a
dominant culture is to have been denominated its other, which means

to carry its least prized attributes." Hite continues, "To be marginal to a dominant culture is also to have little or no say in the construction of one's own socially acknowledged identity" (xv). For this reason, awakenings to limitations, rather than possibilities, predominate in bildungsromans centering on women's lives (Rosowski, 49). Belli's novels insist that the lack of historically visible female antecedents exacerbate the pain of awakening to limitations. She suggests that knowledge of these would offer an affirmation of women's identity as part of a collective as well as a sense of solidarity.

Belli couples her concern with identity with a preoccupation with maternity. She consistently highlights the felt absence of a mother (negative/past) and women's reproductive power in the conception and bearing of children (positive/future). Each protagonist suffers the absence of caring relationships with her parents during formative moments, and the search for the mother is represented as fundamental to the protagonist's definition of self. Her search for identity entails the initial defiance of a male figure of authority (boyfriend, surrogate father, husband, grandfather) and involves an erotic and personal awakening for the woman as the story progresses.

As she confronts questions of identity and history, Belli creates new images of women to replace those constructed and assigned to them by male authorities. Reflecting the weight traditional roles carry in society, her protagonists are persistently aware of themselves as centers of intersecting claims, nations, and identities. The presence (or knowledge) of female antecedents emerges as a source of empowerment for the women negotiating these struggles. According to sociologist Nancy Chodorow, female antecedents have a tremendous impact on a girl's development of her identity, which follows a pattern different from that of boys. Chodorow's studies on the development of a girl's gender identity are particularly relevant to the interpretation of Belli's novels. Chodorow asserts that a girl's "later identification with her mother is embedded in and influenced by their on-going relationship of both primary identification and pre-Oedipal attachment."

Since the girl sustains a "genuine relationship" to her mother as a person, her "gender and gender role identification are mediated by and depend upon real affective relations," and she develops a "personal identification with her mother's general traits and values" (52). The women of Belli's novels lack a maternal presence, and they seek a "mother," a woman with whom to identify and upon whose "general traits of character and values" they might realize and affirm their own subjectivity. Offering an allegory for the search of many contemporary feminists, the novels show a protagonist in search of an inspiring past (or at least a more accurate history than the one she has learned) that will ground her present action.

Does the search for "motherlines" in Belli's fictions have any implications for the interpretation of her works? African-American feminist critics, for whom the analysis of fictional reconstruction of motherlines has been a topic of interest, provide some provocative ideas. For instance, Susan Willis posits, "For black women, history is a bridge defined along motherlines. It begins with a woman's particular genealogy and fans out to include all female culture heroes . . . , as well as political activists" (817). For black women of twentieth-century America, the journey can retrace the transition from an agrarian to an urban society, with its accompanying effects on individual and collective identity. The reconstruction includes popular icons to facilitate a consciousness of resistance and a sense of empowerment. In Belli there is no tracing of motherlines but rather a confrontation of their absence and the imperative of their recollection. Unlike the black women of contemporary African-American fiction, Belli's privileged, bourgeois protagonists do not have mothers with whom they can identify. Why? Each has either broken abruptly from the past, thus rejecting her origins, or simply does not know her own story because of an absent mother.

That Belli would develop such heroines resonates with the recent past of Nicaragua and the experiences of revolutionary women. As I have noted elsewhere, pro-Sandinista writers and cultural workers in

Nicaragua rejected the immediate past, which had been discredited and dismantled by the revolution.[1] In its stead, they employed other raw materials in the construction of a new cultural identity. To establish a new identity, writers frequently glorified revolutionary efforts or idealized a distant, usually indigenous, past. Belli's first novel, *La mujer habitada,* is one such narrative. However, since the revolution involved women in active roles, female militants from traditional middle-class families faced a double rejection of their past. They rejected both bourgeois culture and the image represented by their complicit "mothers" (wives, mothers, and homemakers). Fighting for a place beside their (frequently machista) male comrades, they began to forge alternative womanly ideals.

The recognition of the lack of a female tradition and the imperative of its creation for women's subjectivity is arguably the most salient characteristic of Belli's writings, despite the widely commented political commitment of her earlier works. Kathleen March notes, "In the recent bilingual anthology, *De la costilla de Eva* . . . , Belli takes this position of female empowerment and maintains it throughout the book. Whatever the referent—this specific book, poetry or writing in general, social commitment (all are implied)—it is qualified as *the creation of woman*" (246; emphasis added). In Belli's works there is a preoccupation with the creation of woman, the invention of an identity based on a celebration of women's power, both creative and procreative. This was immediately evident in her early poetry, as in "Y Dios me hizo mujer," from her first volume, *Sobre la grama* (1974). Consider the following fragments:

> Y Dios me hizo mujer,
> de pelo largo,
> ojos,
> nariz y boca de mujer.
> . . . .
> Compuso mi sangre

y me inyectó con ella
para que irrigara
todo mi cuerpo;
nacieron así las ideas,
los sueños,
el instinto. (reprinted in *El ojo, 3*)

[And God made me woman, with the long hair, eyes, nose, and mouth of a woman. . . . He made my blood and injected me with it so that it would irrigate my whole body; thus were born ideas, dreams, instinct.] This poem celebrates the female body and mind, appropriating and redeploying the signs for sensuality and intelligence that in patriarchal Latin American society signal temptation, evil, or menace to men. In "Y Dios me hizo mujer," there is no male gaze to construct a dangerous and tempting Other; there is rather a self-contemplation in which the female speaker revels in her identity as a woman. Other poetry by Belli, such as "Sencillos deseos" and "Furias para danzar" in *De la costilla de Eva* (1986) similarly affirm a female identity developed in active dialogue with the male addressee of the poems. Additionally, Belli frequently locates both interlocutors within the context of war, death, and separation, grounding her erotic celebrations in the reality of Central America.

As in the earlier poetry, in *La mujer habitada* the search for place and the centering of the female subject involve a retelling of the past of the protagonist and the isthmus. The roots of the protagonist Lavinia's rebellion are linked to those of her indigenous predecessor, Itzá, who comes to inhabit her body and motivate her integration into the liberation movement of Faguas.[2] The psychological centering comes from an identification with the revolutionary movement. Furthermore, confidence in the ability of the revolution to interpret reality gives this novel a tightly developed story line.

Belli's other two novels feature protagonists with interior dilemmas similar to those of Lavinia. However, the resolution of their conflicts is not the comparatively facile one of revolutionary integration and identification. The allegory of a woman's search for a female tradition is strikingly obvious in *Sofía de los presagios,* as it takes as the central figure of the story the abandoned daughter of gypsy parents. The search for the mother is again the quest, the realization of which will lead to a centering of the subject who has herself become a mother. In *Waslala* the same theme appears, with the protagonist, Melisandra, engaged in a journey to find her parents in the utopia they were supposed to have helped found and continue to inhabit. In *Waslala,* Melisandra's discovery of her mother leads to both relief and disappointment, which culminate in the protagonist's renewed dedication to her position as a leader.

The quest for a female tradition is visible as a driving force in each of the three novels analyzed here. Though I do not address it explicitly, Belli's poetry also engages in the same reconstruction of female identity, centered in eroticism, maternity, and political/cultural activity. The first novel, *La mujer habitada,* reaches beyond the immediate past to find an indigenous antecedent for the twentieth-century protagonist. The story also raises several questions about the depiction of subalternity and revolution in the fictionalized history. Belli's second novel, *Sofía de los presagios,* is not a historical novel per se, but it shares the same preoccupation with a women's history in a post-revolutionary context. A futuristic endeavor, *Waslala* considers the future of women and the isthmus. Another woman, a matriarchal figure of a new sort, occupies the center of this drama, pursuing her mother and a lost utopia in a globalized world of exploitation and war.

Women, Subalterns, and Revolution in La mujer habitada

The search for a women's tradition and the affirmation of a female erotic combine in *La mujer habitada* as the story of revolutionary *concientización* and triumph. Unlike other Central American texts from the same period, the novel strikes a tenuous balance between a celebration of the revolution and a criticism of its shortcomings. If the pro-Sandinista literature of the revolutionary struggle and the incipient administration in the 1980s projected a vision of what the revolution would mean for the people of Nicaragua, *La mujer habitada* problematized that which it came to be. It at once celebrates the ideal proposed by the Sandinista revolution and deconstructs its paternalistic and romantic idealism by means of a displacement of the events to the fictional nation of Faguas. Written and published relatively late in the revolutionary process, the work shows the fissures in the revolutionary project from within, questioning especially the role of women in revolutionary society.

La mujer habitada first appeared in 1988, published by Editorial Vanguardia in Nicaragua. From the beginning, it generated considerable critical interest and achieved wide popular circulation. In 1992 it was already in its twelfth Spanish edition and had been translated into several languages. Though the revolutionary moment it considers is past, the novel merits critical analysis, particularly because it focuses on issues of gender in a significant historical period.

La mujer habitada intentionally develops bridges between two distinct historical epochs to show the continuity of the oppression of women as well as their struggle to assert themselves as subjects and not objects of historical events. The text attempts to recover the history of the subaltern and the marginalized in order to affirm a women's tradition and to celebrate the political revolution that would liberate oppressed groups. However, as Gramsci notes (54–55), to find continuity in the subaltern's history is a difficult, if not impossible task, and the reading of the subaltern, the woman, and the revolution proposed by *La mujer habitada* is a problematical one.

If the reader approaches the text complicitly, he sympathizes with the revolution and participates in the process of concientización. As Arias notes of Central American narrative, "Los autores desean transformar a su lector ideal en una especie de activista que debe participar de las opciones que se presentan, en vez de responder como un ente pasivo sin poder de decisión" ("Conciencia," 43) [The authors want to transform their ideal reader into a sort of activist who should participate in the choices presented, instead of having him respond as a passive being with no decision-making power]. In the case of *La mujer habitada,* the unique structure of the novel and the mesmerizing employment of violence work to convert the reader from passive reception to active identification with the protagonist and her struggle. This is a common strategy in most leftist writing from Central America from the same period; what distinguishes Belli from other writers is her emphasis on the problems of women within revolutionary society. Henry Cohen pointed out in his study of the novel that "Belli's originality in the context of *sandinismo* is to have constructed a fictional antecedent ... who can serve as a model for contemporary women" (42).

Read one way, the story is a proposal for the subaltern's history, presenting the life and actions of the "resisting woman" in a coherent narrative. It is the first of Belli's three novels to dramatize the need for a women's history, and it creates a mythico-historical, female antecedent to serve as a guide for women in a struggle for personal and national liberation. This is the way most critics have read *La mujer habitada.* Nevertheless, the novel is full of textual tensions that hint at more provocative themes, at least for the purposes of my project. The novel explicitly recuperates women's history; it also implicitly reveals the difficulties of doing so.

La mujer habitada posits an intimate relationship between the indigenous woman and the modern protagonist, who experiences a political awakening. To explain the situation in which Lavinia, the protagonist, finds herself, the novel deals with two distinct historical periods: the Conquest and the revolutionary struggle of the 1970s in Central America. A second subaltern subject, Itzá (the spirit of an Indian woman), facilitates the incorporation of events of the Conquest into the novel.

A young architect who works in the capital of Faguas, Lavinia does not actively seek her past but rather gradually becomes aware of its significance. Rebellious in the face of the social expectations of her bourgeois parents, she begins to recognize the injustices of her country and joins the revolutionary front in armed struggle for national liberation. Itzá appears in the text as the reincarnation of a young Indian woman who fought beside her lover during the Conquest and died in the indigenous resistance against the Spanish invaders. When the novel begins, Itzá has just been regenerated in the orange tree that grows in the patio of Lavinia's home. Her spirit penetrates Lavinia's body by means of the juice Lavinia prepares from the fruits of the tree. In this way the metaphor of the "inhabited woman" is born. With the help of her warrior ancestor, Lavinia carries out the unfinished resistance against a dominant culture that is oligarchic, machista, and violently oppressive.

By interpreting the revolution from the perspective of two women, the text communicates a series of alliances, oppositions, and conflicts to create a vision of a dynamic and contested revolutionary culture. Both female subjects, Lavinia and Itzá, negotiate their existences and identities amid the competing claims of ideologies and patriarchies, finding that each time they act they are marginalized by mechanisms of the dominant culture. Itzá is marginalized in the sixteenth century not only because she is a member of the indigenous culture subjugated by the Spanish but also because she is a woman in the indigenous patriarchy. Lavinia's situation is similar in that she cannot find her place in either of the two social options readily available to her. Because she is an independent, single woman, she is marginalized by the machista culture prevalent in the streets, offices, and homes of Faguas, even though her upper-class status spares her from socioeconomic marginalization. However, her privileged position in Faguan society makes her feel alienated among the liberation front revolutionaries, who do not share the same experiences as she because of class differences.

The narrative strategies of the novel reflect the complex negotiations of the plot. Two juxtaposed narratives alternate in the text to develop Lavinia's story. Although the heterodiegetic-extradiegetic narrative is the principal one, this and the other (narrated by Itzá) interpenetrate to such a degree that as the novel approaches its violent climax the distinctions between them are minimalized.

The principal narrative presents the story of Lavinia's incorporation into the revolutionary movement. It employs almost constant focalization to relay the thoughts and soliloquies of Lavinia. As Amy Kaminsky has observed, the principal narrative is a realistic narrative—specifically, a bildungsroman (19). According to David Lloyd, the bildungsroman is traditionally "the tale of an individual's passage from singularity to social integration. The anomalous individual learns to be reconciled with society and its projects" (755–56). In *La mujer habitada* Belli appropriates this novelistic form for revolutionary and feminist ends. In her story the rebellious individual is a woman who does not integrate herself into the hegemonic social order but rather into the leftist vanguard that seeks to inaugurate another social order. Furthermore, Lavinia's self-criticism fills focalized passages about her development as a revolutionary subject. The text makes visible the mechanisms that transform people like Lavinia and also leads the reader to believe that Lavinia recognizes her own motives and the process that changes her. For instance, Lavinia questions her motives in her amorous and revolutionary involvement, examining the extent to which she participates in the expectations of that discriminatory society she seeks to destroy.

The text not only appropriates the bildungsroman to tell the story of a guerrillera; it also subverts the genre at the discursive level. Besides its realistic dimension, *La mujer habitada* includes an alternative, magical narrative whose progression locates the principal narrative in a different interpretive context. History, then, is not simply a linear progression toward utopia but a cyclical series of events that lend mythical significance to the choices and actions of Lavinia. The combination of narratives produces tension in the work: for its own significative process, the text depends on the very norms of representation that it intends to subvert. Thus, we can affirm with Arias (who in turn echoes M. M. Bakhtin) that this discourse "imita el discurso dominante en su aspiración a ganar poder, apropiándose del mismo. Por el otro, desnuda—carnivaliza—ese mismo discurso" ("Descolonizando," 74) [imitates the dominant discourse in its aspiration to gain power, appropriating the discourse for itself. On the other hand, it strips bare—carnivalizes— that same discourse]. In its retelling of Sandinista revolutionary activity in the early 1970s, the text appropriates a thoroughly European form, but the double voice of the text reinterprets the form to use its power for other ideological ends.[3]

The voice of Itzá offers the alternative, magical discourse that interrupts the flow of the principal narrative. The first-person narrator observes Lavinia at the same time that she participates with her at the diegetic level. Since Itzá is a mythical entity not subject to human spacio-temporal exigencies, she enjoys a privileged position; she is at once observer of and participant in Lavinia's story. Her discourse is comprised of observations of Lavinia and a series of anecdotes about Itzá's own experiences as a woman. These analepses integrate the story of the Conquest into the story of contemporary revolution. The secondary narrative thus locates the trajectory of Lavinia's life, which follows a linear development, from concientización to liberation, within a cyclical conception of history. At the same time that it affirms her life, it emphasizes the continuity of the struggle and finally denies a utopian vision of revolutionary triumph.

The connection that is developed between Lavinia and Itzá is a nexus central to Belli's invention of a women's history. Like the text itself, Lavinia is a site of conflict between several opposing forces: political, social, and cultural. In the text, she does not represent a particular program or ideology but rather is an individual in search of her identity and historical subjectivity. In this search, Itzá plays the role of the mythical and revolutionary antecedent who is able to inspire the protagonist.

As Belli elaborates the relationship between Itzá and Lavinia, she establishes several metaphoric and metonymic associations to gain the complicity of the reader and guide his interpretation of the revolution. As in other leftist texts from Central America, the protagonist of *La mujer habitada* has her conscience awakened. She is then pushed toward political engagement in a slow process that involves a closer identification with el pueblo and eventual commitment to the revolutionary movement. As it describes this process, the text invites the reader to identify with the protagonist and to understand that the brutal injustice of dictatorship permits no response other than armed struggle.

However, *La mujer habitada* intertwines the creation of a subaltern history with the plot of concientización. The most important strategy in depicting the revolution as an act of liberation is the association made between the modern struggle against dictatorship and indigenous resistance during the Conquest. Through the observations of Itzá and the juxtaposition of the two narratives in the same text, the novel insistently develops a link between indigenous resistance and twentieth-century revolution. According to this representation, the female protagonists share a common resistance in the face of exploitative and abusive systems, which are in turn identified with patriarchal domination. Belli thus suggests that contemporary Central American reality is the legacy of a colonial program of subjugation and extermination. The similarity between the women's experiences points out the continuity of gender-based discrimination that makes the subaltern woman doubly alienated.

In the text, Itzá is the link that connects the twentieth-century conflict with another epoch, thus lending narrative logic to events separated by centuries of history. The memories offered in the analepsis of Itzá emphasize the difficulties women have encountered when they attempt to become historical agents, no matter the social or political system. According to the text, just because she is a woman, Lavinia is forced to adjust to the same prejudices that Itzá faced during the Conquest, five centuries before. The stories of Itzá reconstruct the narrative of the subaltern's history, linking the dilemma of Lavinia with that of her mythical antecedent to project a narrative continuity that official history does not recognize.

There are signals throughout *La mujer habitada* that invite the reader to see Lavinia's problems as a continuation of the history of the life of Itzá. For example, the first passage to describe Lavinia begins this way: "El día que floreció el naranjo, Lavinia se levantó temprano para ir a trabajar por primera vez en su vida" (11) [The day the orange tree blossomed Lavinia got up early to go to work for the first time in her life]. Both women take on new roles in life; Itzá begins a new existence in the orange tree, and Lavinia begins her professional career. Even before the "inhabitation" of Lavinia's body by the spirit of Itzá, there were similarities established between the two women. The identification is sealed when Itzá enters Lavinia's body. The inhabitation itself suggests the penetration of the magical and the supernatural into the "real" world; it blurs the lines between everyday life and a magical alterity.

It is Itzá who functions as a mythical female predecessor for Lavinia. She is the actant that lends mythological legitimacy to the guerrilla struggle, just as the figure of Sandino did in the Sandinista movement in Nicaragua. Consider the following passage, which describes a dream Lavinia had when she went to the mountains for her guerrilla training: "Soñó que estaba con un vestido de grandes flores blancas y amarillas en un lugar como una fortaleza. Tenía en la mano una pistola extraña que parecía cañón en miniatura. Desde atrás, una mujer con trenzas le ordenaba disparar" (265) [I dreamed I was wearing a dress with big white and yellow flowers in a place like a fort. I had a strange pistol in my hand that was like a miniature cannon. From behind, a woman with braids ordered me to shoot]. Clearly, the female figure conjured here in Lavinia's dream represents a mythical antecedent for the struggle of the modern guerrillera. The text leaves her identity uncertain, though she could easily be Rafaela Herrera Mora, a young woman who fought against the British attack on the

Castillo de la Concepción on the San Juan River in 1762.[4] Whether the dream figure is Itzá or Herrera, the intention of Belli is the same: to create a female figure that corresponds to Sandino and that will serve as forebear and guide to women in the movement.

As the dream insinuates, Lavinia's struggle is not only against the dictator but also against all oppressors of the people throughout history. The juxtaposition of the history of the Conquest with modern events contextualizes the dictator in a legacy of repression and associates him with the brutality of the conquerors. The metonymic relation (*el Gran General* = the historically exploitative patriarchy) makes the dictator guilty not just of the atrocities of his own regime but also of all abuses perpetrated against the people since the arrival of the Europeans. Belli sometimes falls into the trap of simplifying complex situations in the style of the Black Legend, but she does construct an image of resistance that has been building over time.[5] To show the persistence of the oppression thus gives continuity to the history of the resisting subaltern. In this way, to topple the dictator means putting an end to centuries of abuse, and the effort to do so becomes a moral imperative in the text.

Combining the two narratives, the novel proposes a reading of reality that differs from traditional representations of history as a narrative about events, parties, and states. At the same time, the work presents a vision of historical processes motivated by forces outside the traditional centers of power. This vision proceeds from the focus on subaltern subjects whose history is, according to Gramsci, "necessarily fragmented." Belli's text makes an effort to recover and reconstruct the historical continuity of the subaltern's resistance by employing an alternative discourse. To inaugurate another social and political order, the novel suggests that one must invent or intuit subaltern history.

However, there are certain problems with the project in the novel. Curiously, Itzá has a great deal in common with the mestiza, bourgeois woman in the twentieth-century capital of Faguas. Of course, there are certain experiences that the two women could easily have in common, for example, the social marginalization they both endure as women. Nevertheless, there is little mention of differences that would certainly exist between a sixteenth-century indigenous woman and a twentieth-century woman of a different cultural heritage. Here it is useful to remember the protests of women like Domitila Barrios de Chungara in *Si me permiten hablar* (1977) and Maria Lugones and Elizabeth Spelman in "Have We Got a Theory for You!" In this latter article, the Hispanic voice of Lugones admonishes the Anglo feminist: "You do have an obligation to abandon your imperialism, your universal claims, your reduction of us to your selves" (576). Domitila Barrios, activist wife of a Bolivian miner, said much the same to a group of Mexican feminists she met at a United Nations–sponsored conference on women. Each time feminists consider what it means to be a woman, voices like these remind women that all people have identities determined by their respective cultures and that this diversity affects solidarity based on sex and gender. How far does *La mujer habitada* go in blurring differences between women? In whose image is the indigenous antecedent, the imagined mother, created? In the service of what ideology?

In the novel, the representation of the subaltern serves a revolutionary ideology and lends it mythical legitimacy. Itzá's narrative decentralizes the text in discursive terms, but the first-person narration has the principal function of complementing the story of Lavinia and confirming the reader's conjectures about events in Lavinia's life. Itzá's narrative emphasizes the conflicts and difficulties Lavinia encounters in negotiating her own space in dictatorial and revolutionary Faguas. Even at the beginning of the story, when Itzá does not know Lavinia, the deductions of Itzá guide the reader in elaborating and evaluating the protagonist. From the first we see the development of Itzá's impressions, which communicate at once more and less than what we surmised from the primary narrative: "Vi una mujer. . . . Tiene rasgos parecidos a las mujeres de los invasores, pero también el andar de las mujeres de la tribu" (*Mujer,* 11) [I saw a woman. . . . She has features similar to those of the wives of the invaders, but also the gait of the women of the tribe]. This passage makes us privy to Lavinia's ethnic background, but it also suggests the hybrid nature of the protagonist, the most salient characteristic of Lavinia throughout the text. Like Itzá, Lavinia always finds herself between two opposed worlds. The text employs Itzá's narrative to emphasize this quality in Lavinia and to highlight each opposition: Indian/Spanish, passive/ active, bourgeois/revolutionary, complicity/resistance.

But for this twentieth-century woman in search of her identity, does Itzá exist? Does the recuperation of the past have any effect on the present reality of women like Itzá? And what implication do the answers to those questions have for the interpretation of the novel? Although Lavinia's female comrade reminds her that "después de todo, lo indígena, lo llevamos en la sangre" (239) [after all, we carry our indigenous past in our blood], for both of them, the Indian heritage of their country only surfaces in relation to the political struggles of the revolutionary front.

Throughout the novel, one senses the presence of the indigenous subaltern, but she infiltrates Lavinia's world only subtly. She bursts to the forefront only in the climax. In that scene, the spirit of Itzá impels Lavinia to pull the trigger and assassinate the dictator. In some sense, then, the indigenous past does impact the present, but the words Itzá narrates indicate that her role is principally metaphorical and mythical: "Ni ella ni yo hemos muerto sin designio ni herencia. Volvimos a la tierra desde donde de nuevo viviremos. Poblaremos de frutos carnosos el aire de tiempos nuevos" (387) [Neither she nor I have died without a purpose or a legacy. We returned to the earth from which we will come to life again. We will populate new times with succulent fruits]. Although the novel attempts to emphasize and vindicate the indigenous presence in Faguas, there is no evidence of an indigenous presence in actuality. First Itzá and then Lavinia belong to legends that give life to the revolution.

The conclusion of the novel presents a difficulty for recuperating alternative histories and points again to the textual tensions apparent in the work. At the plot level, there is a protagonist extraordinarily conscious and critical of herself. Similarly, Belli offers a hybrid text that reveals her own confrontation with strategies of representation. To tell a love story in which a woman becomes involved in the political movement to which her boyfriend belongs would be to produce another text to add to the volumes that posit a passive role for women, adding to it only an ideological message. Therefore, the text wavers, presenting a woman who is the site of conflicting forces but still acting on her own initiative. The text also intertwines a "realistic" plot in the principal narrative with a magical and supernatural perspective that "interferes" in the development of the story. Lavinia's story is both a romance and a revolutionary bildungsroman about the process of awakening. The narrative of Itzá decentralizes the text as it presents a magical world, foreign to our generally accepted interpretations of reality. Nevertheless, the story of Itzá does not belong to her completely but rather exists to serve a political program (feminism? national liberation?) that will presumably vindicate her through revolutionary triumph.

But is revolutionary triumph the panacea for all the ills Faguas suffers? It seems that the author, intentionally or not, expresses certain doubts in the conclusion of the novel. Also, by presenting Lavinia's self-conscious criticism in key moments, the text incorporates within itself the semantic seeds of its own destruction. By recognizing textually the criticisms that could be made about the ideology it espouses, the text moves between an unmasking and an affirmation of its discourse. As Kaminsky notes, all this has as its object the seduction of the reader (21), but I believe that so much tension focalized in the protagonist is significant for other reasons as well.

I have already noted that Lavinia is an individual in search of a historical subjectivity and that she is a site of conflict for opposing forces of politics, class, and culture. For these reasons, she feels marginalized. In the society of her conservative parents, Lavinia is marginalized for her feminism and her independence. Her parents have traditional expectations for her; they send her to Europe to study and hope that she will return to marry a respectable man from her own social class. When she opts to live in the house that her spinster aunt left to her, her relationship with her parents becomes more difficult. However, in the company of her leftist comrades, Lavinia is marginalized precisely because of her social class. The following quote from the text is particularly significant: "A pesar de la aceptación que el Movimiento le brindaba, [Lavinia] no dejaba de sentir su clase como un fardo pesado del que hubiera querido liberarse de una vez por todas. Le parecía una culpa sin perdón; una frontera que quizás sólo la muerte heroica podría desvanecer totalmente" (294) [Despite the acceptance that the Movement gave her, Lavinia never stopped feeling that her social class was a burden from which she would have liked to have been freed once and for all. To her, it was an unpardonable guilt; a barrier that perhaps only a heroic death could eliminate completely]. The text thus begins insinuating that in the culture that will ultimately triumph in Faguas, Lavinia will not have a place either. The only way to resolve the identity crisis she experiences is to sacrifice herself and allow history to give her the stable identity of revolutionary martyr. And this is precisely what happens. Lavinia dies, sacrificing herself and leaving the leftist utopia to those who fit perfectly in the new revolutionary society. Thus are resolved the tensions of the plot, but the implications of such a resolution are unsettling. They are also central to the interpretation of the text.

As the book concludes, the two guerrillas of bourgeois origin die in the assault on the general's house. Lavinia's childhood friend Pablo dies at the beginning of the attack, and Lavinia also perishes. Earlier during the same evening of the assault, Lavinia's machista boyfriend, Felipe, died also. Only those who easily fit in the new hegemonic culture of the revolution remain. The difficulties disappear in this imagined world: "El mediador se había llevado la propuesta. Se negociaría. 'Eureka' había salido bien. Mañana todo habría terminado" (386) [The mediator had taken the proposal. They would negotiate. The revolutionary action, "Eureka" had turned out well. Tomorrow everything would be over]. This vision is a pleasing one and perhaps necessary for textual closure, but it eliminates the complexity of the revolution and the society that its leaders attempted to create after the victory.

It is significant that in *La mujer habitada* neither Lavinia nor Itzá fits into the system offered them by society. Both managed to maneuver their ways into male society in work and in war. Both defied societal norms for women in amorous relationships, rejecting the prescribed passivity and suffering the disapprobation of their respective cultures. And although the conclusions of their struggles are different—Lavinia's cause triumphs while Itzá's obviously did not—neither of the two women survives to see the dawn of the new social order. Since both women die before reaching their goals, the text suggests that they do not fit in the new reality but rather belong to a mythical space that legitimizes it.

The truth is that not all the machistas nor the bourgeois perished in the struggle and that there was and is a very real indigenous presence in Nicaragua. All these groups remained after the war to become a part of the new regime, to form part of the counterrevolutionary forces, or to leave the country as exiles. For women like Daisy Zamora, Gioconda Belli, and many others who participated in the fight for a new Nicaragua, the triumph of the revolution and its enthusiasm for redrawing sociocultural lines and borders caused intimate and personal crises. Read in this light, *La mujer habitada* is indeed a novel that tells the history of women. Better yet, it is a novel that reveals the difficulty that representing the history of the margins presents for the author and reader. As others have commented, we can also agree that the novel is a testimonial one, not just of the Christmas assault of 1974 but of the struggle of the marginalized subject—woman or Indian—to find and assert her identity in any society.

Daughters Seeking Mothers:
Sofía de los presagios *and* Waslala

Like *La mujer habitada,* the second and third novels of Gioconda Belli focus on women's struggles to establish their identities in a world where they must constantly resist becoming objects. Unlike *La mujer habitada,* neither *Sofía de los presagios* nor *Waslala* attempts to construct mythical female antecedents or a subaltern history that corresponds to revolutionary ideals. They have also received significantly less critical attention. Part of this can be attributed to a shift in interests in the academy and part to less accomplished narrative art in the two novels.

Despite some technical deficiencies, the two novels offer insights on the subject of women's history and their struggle for identity. Both novels center on the conscious desire of contemporary women to know and understand their own history, which for Belli is consistently represented by an absent mother. In canonical Western literature, the search for the mother is a plot that is generally suppressed; the male-centered Oedipal myth is the predominant narrative about the quest for identity and self. In *Sofía de los presagios* and *Waslala,* Belli manipulates Oedipal and quest narratives to serve a feminist agenda.

Historically, rite-of-passage and heroic quest narratives have been male-centered dramas. Women in these tales are usually either props or property, rarely actors. In *Sofía* and *Waslala,* Belli conserves some of the formulas of the bildungsroman and heroic quest, but her employment of female protagonists necessitates modification of the genre. Her texts follow the same basic pattern of development of a young protagonist, but the central preoccupation is with the woman as "misfit," or orphan, or outsider because of her refusal to conform to gender stereotypes. As Belli turns from the overtly political tone of *La mujer habitada,* her central preoccupation with identity and memory persists.

In Belli's later novels, as in *La mujer habitada,* divergences from dominant narratives reveal contested spaces in contemporary culture. For instance, *Sofía* superficially resembles the bildungsroman. It follows the protagonist from a position of alienation, through a period of crisis, to her final integration into society as an adult who appreciates the lessons learned from experience. Like other woman-centered bildungsromans, however, it features an awakening to limits rather than possibilities. The novel centers on the protagonist's reaction to those limits and her fight to achieve a space for self-expression.

In *Sofía,* traditional tropes and structures are reworked to serve new significative aims. The story begins with Sofía as a child and follows her into early adulthood and maternity, and the representation of these stages is significant. Sofía's childhood is briefly encapsulated in several chapters at the beginning, and then she is married. Usually a climactic moment in fiction, the marriage takes place early in the story and represents the initiation of a crisis for Sofía, rather than a resolution of tension.

The turning point of the story is the escape of Sofía from her confinement as the passively rebellious, cloistered wife of René. This episode alone reveals several innovations. In it, the protagonist trades the weapons of the weak for active rebellion. She flees by night and ascends the volcano Mombacho to seek refuge with Xintal, a healer who becomes her mentor and friend. The episode could easily be dismissed as a melodramatic rendition of the familiar trope of ascension and retreat, employed in everything from biblical myths to Omar Cabezas's *La montaña es algo más que una inmensa estepa verde* (1982). Like other heroes who ascend the mountain in order to emerge transformed, Sofía forges a new determination and sense of self in the days she spends on Mombacho. According to Belli's model of transformation, however, the protagonist does not develop under the supervision of a revolutionary *comandante,* which implies a hierarchical relationship and the perpetuation of authority. Rather, she learns under the tutelage of a female mentor (generally regarded as a witch in the community of Diriá) who becomes her confidante and friend. Though the portrayal of Xintal's summit abode is at times clichéd, it represents an appropriation of the myth of ascension, retreat, and initiation in knowledge, this time for feminist ends.

Sofía de los presagios, like *La mujer habitada,* appropriates the bildungsroman to tell tales of revolutionary and feminist empowerment. *Waslala* adapts another form—the heroic quest—to tell of a woman's search for her past, as well as her place in the future. Like many a hero of Western lore, the young, attractive protagonist of *Waslala* must leave the protection of family and homeland in a perilous journey in search of utopia. However, the dangers she encounters are those of a globalized world: drug lords, nuclear accidents, and opportunistic envoys from wealthier, more developed regions. In the new world order, Belli's fundamental concern is again identity. The heroine, Melisandra, seeks her mother and the community her mother founded with other artists and poets. Only in finding these, she believes, can she find her role in Faguas's troubled present.

The search for female solidarity and particularly for a strong mother-daughter relationship is central to the plots of both *Sofía de los presagios* and *Waslala.* The heroines break with the male objects of affection and identification in order to seek their missing mothers, whose presence it is hoped will ground their identity as women. In the search for their history, they seek out relationships with others who have faced similar struggles and the same oppression. As Adrienne Rich has asserted, stories like Belli's are not frequently heard in Western society: "This cathexis between mother and daughter—essential, distorted, misused—is the great unwritten story. Probably there is nothing in human nature more resonant with charges than the flow of energy between two biologically alike bodies.... The materials are there for the deepest mutuality and the most painful estrangement.... Yet this relationship has been minimized and trivialized in the annals of patriarchy" (225-26). This connection between mother and daughter is explored in both *Sofía* and *Waslala.*

Unlike the protagonist of *La mujer habitada* (who remains ignorant of the woman that gives her strength), the heroines of *Sofía* and *Waslala* actively seek their mothers and desire to base their identities on identification with them (rather than separation, as in the Oedipus myth). There are no mythical antecedents in the two novels, no self-sacrificing heroines of revolution, no narratives of macropolitical liberation. Rather, there is a concern with the recuperation of an intimate history that will anchor the nascent subjectivities of women.

The recuperation of the memory and history of the mother represented in Belli's novels is particularly significant in the light of Luce Irigaray's assessment of Western culture as inherently matricidal.[6] There are certainly abundant examples of this matricidal tendency in Belli's Spanish and Latin American literary antecedents. Mothers in dramas of the Spanish golden age are dead, invisible, unnamed, and unknown. They are also noticeably absent in nineteenth-century romantic novels such as Jorge Isaacs's *María* (1867) and the realist texts that followed. Twentieth-century Latin American literary culture through the Boom offers only a slight improvement, assembling the same figures of Eve, La Malinche, and the Virgin Mary as maternal types.[7]

Belli's more immediate literary antecedents—Boom authors—replicated the same stereotypes about mothers as well. According to Debra Castillo, most damaging is their denial of subjectivity to mothers, a modern variation, perhaps, of matricide:

> The "Boom" writers of the 1960s and 1970s, who deconstructed and resemanticized so many of the meaning systems of official mythology, seem to have been oblivious to the degree to which they reaffirmed the myth of the maternal body as equivalent to a state of nature and of maternal "nature" as an unproblematic concept. . . . In all these works, the maternal body may be a utopian site, but the mother's lack of access to subjectivity is a nonnegotiable given. (23)

If the mother is present in Boom literature, then, she certainly does

73

not feel, think, or act—making her a very poor model for women who want to assert themselves in society.

Belli's texts actively seek to reclaim the mother: to give her textual presence and a voice. They confront head-on the matricidal tradition in Western culture, one that women like Belli faced not only in the "foundational fictions" of their cultures, but also in their efforts to become writers. As Maureen Shea has noted, women have suffered a lack of "literary mothers" to serve as guides and models (101). Only since the 1960s has the recuperation of women's textual traditions been the collective endeavor of feminist historians and critics. Like these feminists, Belli's protagonists undertake the search for the missing mother, attempting to ground their identities, desires, and places in society in ways other than those offered to them by patriarchal social structures.

In *Sofía* the protagonist becomes obsessed with possessing a memory of her mother. Her inquietude reaches crisis proportions late in her pregnancy with her first child. She is not satisfied until she dreams of her mother and can retain a mental image of her; then she declares herself well, and Xintal notes that "ya tiene ombligo" (221) [now she has a navel]. An apparently innocuous phrase, Xintal's statement evokes pre-Columbian understandings of the earth and humanity, as well as images of fertility and cycles of life. After this dream, Sofía has a sign of her origins, her connectedness to another human being, and her position in a cycle of endlessly repeating history. Also, according to the text, from this point on she has a different image of her "cuerpo deforme" (deformed body—deformed from pregnancy) and is able to act with reasoned determination.

The representation of the mother-daughter bond is unique in *Sofía de los presagios* because it gives voice to the woman-as-mother instead of focusing solely on women's self-identification as daughters.[8] Because the novel is chiefly concerned with Sofía's desire to find her mother and herself, most of the text sustains the image of the mother as the daughter's other. It does, however, include representations of Sofía as mother. Images such as these fill a literary vacuum, according to Marianne Hirsch: "The story of female development, both in fiction and theory, needs to be written in the voice of mothers as well as in that of daughters. It needs to cease mystifying maternal stories, to cease making them objects of a 'sustained quest.' Only in combining both voices, in finding a double voice that would yield a multiple female consciousness, can we begin to envision ways to 'live afresh'" (161). *Sofía* takes a first step by offering a "double voice" and "multiple female consciousness." Nevertheless, there is a distinct division in the story between Sofía-as-daughter and Sofía-as-mother. The decisive moment is when Sofía is able to retain a mental image of her mother from a dream she has had. At that point, she takes on the role of mother to the child she is carrying. Finally, she feels she has both a history and a place; she can look to the future her daughter embodies.

Belli's work often overtly links historical events to women's decisions and attitudes on the subject of childbearing. Belli's insertion of personal reproductive decisions in the representation of the collective (and vice versa) is noteworthy because it blurs the lines between the public and private. She thereby deconstructs a binary that has often worked to the disadvantage of women.

The association between reproductive choices and public events is first evident in *La mujer habitada,* more fully elaborated in *Sofía,* and discernible to a lesser extent in *Waslala.* In *La mujer habitada,* the negation of motherhood by both Lavinia and Itzá is explicitly linked to the political situation. *La mujer habitada* makes the connection obvious in a narrative segment focalized through Lavinia: "Le dolió el vientre. El dolor se convertía paulatinamente en rabia. Rabia desconocida brotando de la imagen de un niño que jamás existiría. ¿Cuántos niños andarían por el éter, pensó, negados de la vida por estos menesteres? ¿Cuántos en América Latina? ¿Cuántos en el mundo? (134) [Her belly ached. The pain slowly turned to anger. An unknown anger pouring from the image of a child that would never exist. How many children wander in the ether, she wondered, denied life because of these obligations? How many in Latin America? How many in the world?]. According to Belli's portrayal, the political has intimate repercussions. Similarly, the personal decisions made by women and their partners have consequences that extend beyond themselves.

In *La mujer habitada,* the revolution is mother, father, child, companion. The cause of national liberation subsumes all else. For instance, at one point in that novel, Lavinia realizes that "el Movimiento representaba la casi totalidad de su vida: su familia, sus amigos" (323) [the Movement represented almost her whole life: her family, her friends]. Belli's early poetry contains similar representations of the revolution, imagining it in terms of creation and procreation. An entity born of the collective effort of comrades, the revolution will in turn give birth to another generation, as in this poem:

> Engendraremos niños
> con el puño cerrado
> y la conspiración, el secreto en los ojos.
> ....
> Engendraremos niños
> por cada hombre o mujer que nos maten. (*El ojo,* 95)

[We will engender children / with closed fists / and conspiracy, secrecy in their eyes. . . . We will engender children / for each man and woman they kill among us]. Ironically, for the protagonist of *La mujer habitada,* the same commitment to revolution leads to a negation of maternity. Both central female characters refuse to become mothers; Itzá refuses to bear slaves for the conquerors, and Lavinia and Felipe feel their hold on existence too precarious to have a child. Though necessary to guarantee a better future for all, the negation of childbearing is represented as a sacrifice forced upon both couples.

The very multiplicity of the representations of maternity Belli offers is a radical move in literature. Until recently, many works constructed maternity as a uniquely desirable state, one that women sought, welcomed, and enjoyed because it was "natural" for them to do so. Woman-centered novels like Belli's refigure notions of maternity, linking them to definitions of history and identity. They thus acknowledge the interaction between private and public realms that male-centered texts often ignore. For Belli's protagonists, maternity is not a biological imperative, but a choice conditioned by personal preferences and historical contingencies. The treatment of this topic in Belli's fictions recovers another aspect of the mother-daughter plot that has until recently been overlooked or obscured in Latin American culture.

Memory, Myth, and the Will to Power

The need for memory and its creation outside the accepted boundaries of official history (familial or national) is a motif in *La mujer habitada, Sofía,* and *Waslala. La mujer habitada* recuperates the story of resisting women in the isthmus in order to offer a revolutionary interpretation of contemporary reality. It creates a myth for female empowerment from the oral traditions about women and mobilizes fragmented memories in the service of new nationalist projects in Sandinismo.

Though it does not demonstrate the same national concerns as *La mujer habitada, Sofía* also recurs to myths of oral history. Indeed, according to Les Field, in *Sofía* Belli "clearly mined the local history and lore of Masaya-Carazo to create an almost self-contained geographic and psychological region of magic and intrigue in which the state becomes irrelevant to local understandings and lives" (238). In Sofía's story, history cannot be recuperated through ordinary means. The protagonist has been severed from the past by the decisions of others, and their choices have made it inaccessible to her. The textual resolution in the novel comes not through the successful "discovery" of Sofía's history but through its creation by means of magical and imaginative intervention.

Waslala, too, validates alternative understandings of existence and recuperates a memory of the utopia many Sandinistas sought. It recalls the hope the revolution inspired, as well as the distance of that dream from the present. The plot also alludes to the legacy of Nicaragua's poets, suggesting that it harbors a strength and hope capable of engendering the future.[9]

In *Waslala* the poetic imagination of Melisandra's grandfather and the willful determination of her grandmother represent a tradition of resistance and hope that has repercussions across time and space. Poetry fuels the idealism of Don José's progeny in the novel. His daughter and her associates founded the community of Waslala, and this in turn stirs the imagination of Faguas's masses. Melisandra subsequently embarks on a search to reach that vanished utopia, only to find that what is important is not its physical being but the hope it represents.

The ending of *Waslala* is significant for the understanding of Belli's fictionalization of history. When Melisandra encounters the failed utopia, she realizes the value of a "fictional" (i.e., constructed) history in captivating the collective imagination and cultivating solidarity and hope. Her mother explains that she remains in the deserted settlement "porque pienso que Waslala, como mito, como aspiración, justifica su existencia.... considero que es imperativo que exista, . . . que continúe generando leyendas" (370) [because I think that Waslala, as myth, as aspiration, justifies its existence.... I think it is imperative that it exist . . . that it continue to generate legends]. Thus, daughter learns from mother the need for poetry and myths—alternative memories—in a politically and socially fragmented world. Significantly, the novel concludes with Melisandra running out once more into that world. *Waslala* thus intimates that fictions of the past record hopes and desires, serving as "memoriales del futuro" [memorials of the future] for the people to whom they belong.

More than any other novelist considered here, Belli invokes the past in the service of a "will to power." All of Belli's protagonists long for the center from which they have been excluded: Lavinia strives to belong to the revolution, Sofía calculates to become a powerful landowner, and Melisandra wants to exert benevolent control over Faguas. Each plot revolves around the centering of the protagonist and attains closure when she reconciles herself to her past and her destiny.[10] The understanding of one's predecessors and their relationship to the present, according to Belli's fictions, enables a new construction of the future.

Appropriating memories of resistance, as well as genres, Belli's novels vacillate between complicity and subversion as they seek to recover what is missing in the story of women. In doing so, they participate in the ongoing transformation of Nicaragua, renovating the form and function of its history from text to text. Taken as a whole, Belli's corpus of writing multiplies the images of the nation in whose history women have been undeniably imbricated but often invisible. From the revolutionary image of the nation in *La mujer habitada,* Belli moves on to *Sofía de los presagios,* in which the nation no longer figures as the locus for power struggle. *Waslala* and *El país bajo mi piel,* as well as the latest poetry of *Apogeo,* navigate the postnational context of globalization, acknowledging and participating in a world of exchange and consumption without borders. In each world, Belli's women urgently seek an alternative, female tradition, a story of mothers and daughters. Her novels undertake the imagination of such a tradition, subtly revealing in their plots its intersections with present realities.

Chapter 3

Asking Other Questions

Personal Stories and Historical Events
in the Fiction of Rosario Aguilar

> To be woman-centered means: asking if women were central to this ar-
> gument, how would it be defined? . . . Women cannot be put into the
> empty spaces of patriarchal thought and systems—in moving to the
> center, they transform the system.
>
> —Gerda Lerner, *The Creation of Patriarchy*

THE STORIES OF most women cannot be found in the public accounts valorized by a male-centered historical record. Rather, as the
novels of Alegría and Belli intimate, they must be discovered between
the lines of texts, in oral traditions and in private writings such as
diaries. Among those Central American writers who have given voice
to alternative histories is Rosario Aguilar. In much of her writing,
Aguilar takes the stories of empires, nations, and men—those fictions
about "the powerful and their doings," in Anna Davin's words—and
posits questions about women (60). This chapter critically examines
the way in which Aguilar reinscribes the story of both women and the
nation. It also considers Aguilar's interrogation of the notions of the
private and the public, which she questions through the narration of
historical events and personal stories.

Rosario Aguilar's narrative relates intimate stories that are fundamentally interconnected with major cultural and historical events in Central America, particularly Nicaragua. Though not overtly feminist texts, the fictions are certainly woman centered, presenting individual female experiences at crucial historical junctures in Central America. In her interrogation of textual and oral traditions from colonial times to the 1990 Sandinista electoral defeat, Aguilar imagines women's lives at particularly significant moments of national history, writing them into a story that their presence there transforms.

Rosario Aguilar in Central American Literature

In Nicaraguan society, more apt to recognize a *poetisa* (poetess) than an *autora* (author), Rosario Aguilar stands out as one of the most prolific and accomplished Nicaraguan novelists, predating the surge in women's writing associated with the revolution. She wrote her first novel, *Primavera sonámbula* (1964), in her twenties, and has continued to publish regularly since. She is also author of *Quince barrotes de izquierda a derecha* (1965), *Rosa Sarmiento* (1968), *Aquel mar sin fondo ni playa* (1970), *Las doce y veintinueve* (1975), *El guerrillero* (1976), *Siete relatos sobre el amor y la guerra* (1986), and *La niña blanca y los pájaros sin pies* (1992).

In the 1990s interest in Aguilar's work increased within Nicaragua and internationally, and in 1999 she became the first woman elected to the Academia Nicaragüense de la Lengua. A 1996 article by Raymond Souza referred to her as "the best writer of prose fiction in Nicaragua" (454), and both Ann González and Nidia Palacios have used feminist theory to study Aguilar's representation of women. Additionally, the translation of *La niña blanca y los pájaros sin pies* published by White Pine Press (under the title *The Lost Chronicles of Terra Firma*) made her work available to English-speaking audiences, particularly in the United States; the novel also had prior distribution in French.[1]

In many of her fictions, especially the later ones, Aguilar directs attention to the stories of women in the Spanish colonies and the nation. In doing so, she breaks centuries of silence and stereotypes about women's roles in these spaces. The dramatis personae of Central American history is overwhelmingly male; women, along with indigenous people and Africans, occupy the peripheries of canonical texts.

In Nicaragua in particular, power has long been associated with politicians and the military, and lack of minority access to these offices has meant textual obscurity for considerable portions of the population. The traditional connection between literature and nation building coupled with the exclusion of women from the public square, virtually eliminated women's presence from historical memory. Furthermore, though some women did write, the public has not viewed their texts as pertinent to national life, relegating them to second-class status. Elizabeth Marchant observes, "Literary traditions that favor national works over those with supposedly personal themes have undoubtedly contributed to the inferior status of writings by women" (7–8). This explains the Nicaraguan acceptance of poetisas, since they work in a genre associated with personal expression rather than the important task of nation building, a topic more appropriate for men to elaborate in epics and novels.

That Rosario Aguilar should write narrative rather than poetry is significant; more so is that she explore precisely those institutionalized biases that have excluded women from the story of the nation. In particular, Aguilar questions a national history that reflects and promotes prejudices against women. As Davin asserts, "The dominant version of history in any society will be one which bolsters the existing situation. . . . Such history will also reflect the general assumptions and concerns of the dominant group. It will embody belief in their superiority. . . . Of course there are other histories . . . , but to let them be heard is not always easy" (60). The dominant version of history in Latin America has long been promulgated by literature as well as historiography. The treatment of historical moments in woman-centered fictions such as those of Aguilar, makes other histories heard in a way that challenges both history and fiction.

Women's Space, National History: Identity, Family, and Crisis

Aguilar's texts focus on issues of identity, sexuality, and maternity, connecting seemingly personal dilemmas to historical moments of rupture and change. All her protagonists are women, and though most are young, she includes several older women in her stories. She also gives representation to different socioeconomic classes. Constant in the stories are questions about identity and place, as well as the frustrations and suffering that result from social injustice, especially that linked to gender or economic position.

Also recurrent in the historical novels is the focus on certain turning points of Central American history—the birth of Rubén Darío in *Rosa Sarmiento,* the 1972 Managua earthquake in *Las doce y veintinueve,* or the Conquest in *La niña blanca y los pájaros sin pies.* In each of these periods of social, cultural, political, and even physical rupture, the veneer of normalcy in society is broken and the inconsistencies of its sustaining myths are made visible. The radical change in society may be accompanied by a shift in women's roles, though a perseverance of their unequal status is equally likely and perhaps more glaringly obvious, given the generalized social disturbance. During each culturally or historically significant moment, however, women's traditional identities as wives, mothers, and daughters face challenges as the patriarchal social structures that dictate their roles experience upheaval. In these moments of crisis, the protagonists of Aguilar's fictional worlds are caught between conformity and desire, complicity and resistance. The novels center about the tension provoked by competing claims on their loyalties and also show the impossibility of women's fulfillment in the societies in which they find themselves. Aguilar's stories link the "grand events" of history, traditionally concerned with political, military, and economic struggles, to issues generally understood as personal, such as sexuality, marriage, and maternity.

Aguilar's historical fiction is strikingly nonlinear, dominated by analepsis, prolepsis, and ambiguous "endings." They are not self-consciously innovative in terms of narrative structure, but they deftly employ focalization and ellipsis. And, unlike many fictions of the same period by well-known authors, the texts do not show the inevitable integration of protagonists into new revolutionary identities in a call to action against injustice. Rather, they use particular strategies to show the small, interior spaces in which the protagonists find themselves and emphasize the continual isolation and internal conflicts felt by each.

My interest here is specifically in the way in which Aguilar reconfigures and transforms the "system" of history as she moves women to the foreground of the narrative. I also examine the spaces inhabited by the female protagonists of Aguilar's historical fiction and especially the problematization of the public/private binary in the telling of woman-centered stories. Recent theories of women's self-representation in texts shed light on the narrative strategies Rosario Aguilar employs to construct her fictions. Julia Kristeva's definition of intertextuality is useful for understanding the manipulation of national discourse in these texts, which Aguilar appropriates and adapts to create her woman-centered vision of history and culture in Central America.

Contested Spaces and the "Maternal Possibility"

In her later fiction, especially *Rosa Sarmiento, Las doce y veintinueve, El guerrillero, Siete relatos,* and *La niña blanca,* Aguilar tells historically based stories that happen on the supposed frontier between the public and private in women's lives. She consistently depicts women's bodies as contested spaces, sites of struggle for power and expression by individual women and by society in general. Her fictions thus show the imbrication of the erotic and the familial in larger social structures. Furthermore, they bring to the foreground the political realities that determine the options of women's self-expression.

The focus on women's experiences and limitations in Central America necessarily introduces previously overlooked elements into literary discourse. Thus, in Aguilar's novels there are what Ann González calls "taboo subjects," (64) such as abortion, marital infidelity, and the rejection of maternity. González rightly points out that Aguilar's writing is significant for its inclusion of these elements. What is most interesting for the purposes of my study, however, is the manner in which Aguilar broaches these subjects in the context of wars, revolutions, exiles, and other national tragedies. She underscores the indivisibility of the public and the private in the story of the past.

The question of motherhood and maternity is of central importance in many of Aguilar's works, both historical and otherwise. Like nothing else, maternity brings into focus the contest over women's bodies and lives. As I consider the particular way in which Aguilar portrays maternity and motherhood, I find it useful here to cite Marilyn Yalom's studies on the subject. Yalom makes a distinction between maternity and motherhood, describing maternity in biological terms as "conception, pregnancy, parturition, lactation, and the nurturing of infants" and motherhood as a social construct involving "the daily care of children and the ensuing lifelong lien on the mother" (5). Based on her reading of European and American women's writing, Yalom asserts that the maternal possibility, as she calls it, is frequently associated in literature with a personal crisis or mental breakdown. The maternal possibility, she says, "forces upon each woman an anguishing confrontation with the most elemental aspects of existence, even if one chooses not to exercise the power of reproduction or if one is physically unable to reproduce" (106). In Aguilar's novels, each woman's reckoning with the maternal possibility occurs in the midst of economic inequality and revolution, and the options available to her link her personal struggles with national concerns "outside" her body. Besides the fundamentally biological challenge with which she is confronted, the protagonist faces a social construction of motherhood proposed by a patriarchal society with little concern for women's subjectivities. Furthermore, a situation of general social upheaval often exacerbates the difficulties faced by the protagonists in the small world of Aguilar's fictions.

Aguilar's depiction of women's struggles with the maternal possibility emphasizes the injustices of both patriarchal expectations and a generally repressive political and economic system. Maternity becomes the space where the public imposition upon women's private desires is realized most dramatically. For numerous protagonists in Aguilar's novels, including Rosa in *Rosa Sarmiento,* the teacher in *El guerrillero,* and María José in *Siete relatos,* maternity provokes a crisis that is both personal and political. In particular, Aguilar's representation of the claims of maternity or motherhood (or both) on bodies and lives reveals the political realities that inform and condition women's choices. And through the presentation of their stories, she deconstructs the public-private binary that has separated the world of women's experience from the male arena of "history."

Aguilar's texts promote a view of maternity similar to that posited by Julia Kristeva. Kristeva has asserted that maternity locates women in an ambiguous position in which they are both a threat to and an assurance of social stability: "If pregnancy is the threshold between nature and culture, maternity is the bridge between singularity and ethics. Through the events of her life, a woman thus finds herself at the pivot of sociality—she is at once the guarantee and the threat to its stability" (297). Because of the potential disorder maternity and motherhood represent for male-dominated society, this "state" of women has historically been highly regulated in social and political terms. Furthermore, Kristeva's interpretation of maternity has a new resonance when applied to Central American reality, where the exertion of individual wills, especially those of women, has been carefully guarded by colonial and national patriarchies apprehensive of any destabilizing forces. The regulation of women's sexuality for reasons of national priority continues to be evident in discussions such as Daniel Ortega's attacks on abortion. In these, the Sandinista leader voiced concerns about "depleting our youth" and provoking a labor shortage (Whisnant, 425). In this and other instances, many male Sandinista leaders were resistant when it came to women's options, not only in the morally controversial area of abortion but also with regard to women's legal rights in the civil and criminal codes specified in the constitution (Whisnant, 430–31).

Aguilar's fiction reveals an acute awareness of women's inequality. She consistently emphasizes that their denial or realization of the maternal possibility is both a personal and a public concern. Though women's participation in national life has been minimized, Aguilar's fictions affirm that they have been present and active in history. Women might have been relegated to the peripheries, as in the Conquest, or to the mythical past of a cultural icon like Darío, but they are intimately involved in the politics of the family and nation.

Moments of rupture, when the often hidden contests over familial and national power are most readily visible, dominate the plots of nearly all her historical novels and novellas. This prompts a couple of questions: If the state is in disarray, as it is in nearly all of Aguilar's historical fiction, how does the family look? What implications does this have for women? As Lerner observes, "the family not merely mirrors the order in the state and educates its children to follow it, it also creates and constantly reinforces that order" (*Creation,* 217). When the family ceases to reinforce that order, what is the result? In moments of national crisis, what are the boundaries of the home, a space most frequently associated with women? What implications do these ruptures have on the identity of individual women? Aguilar's imaginations of particular historical moments allow for the exploration of these issues.

Ensilios *and Ellipses: Desires and Limits in Aguilar's Fictions*

Interestingly, none of the families in *Rosa Sarmiento, El guerrillero, Las doce y veintinueve, Siete relatos,* and *La niña blanca* are integral units. They have no clearly delimited borders. Their boundaries are violated by war and natural disasters, and the women who belong to them live in widely varying circumstances. Despite their social, economic, and political differences, Aguilar consistently associates women with restricted spaces that frustrate their desires for freedom, self-expression, and happiness. Why is this? How do her novels fictionalize moments of historical significance to emphasize again and again the hindrances to female mobility and expression?

Like Jean Franco's *Plotting Women,* Aguilar's texts tell of the "solitary struggle of isolated women," contextualizing their stories within a larger national history to emphasize women's marginality and resistance. Her novels consistently emphasize women's *ensilios,* the psychological and physical confinement felt by women in their own societies. Feminist critic Margaret Higonnet uses the term to refer to "interior exiles": "The repressive force of the family in many societies makes [ensilio] a particularly endemic condition" ("New Cartographies," 13). As in political exile, in the ensilio the individual is kept from participation in the politics and society of her culture, not through any personal volition but rather as a result of repressive forces. What differentiates ensilios from *exilios,* is that women experience interior exiles in their own cultures, which deny them access to political process within the family as well as the nation.

Women who suffer ensilios abound in Aguilar's fictions. Aguilar presents her protagonists as individuals cast in roles they would not have chosen themselves; they are unhappy wives, coerced lovers, reluctant mothers. Consistently denied the agency that would allow them to contribute to the political and cultural world, the women imagine insurrections that would allow them to achieve fulfillment, though most of their plots never reach fruition. That Aguilar locates their dilemmas within historically crucial moments serves to bring into focus the alienation of women within the dramas of national life.

The recurrence of small spaces and internal dialogues in Aguilar's narrative points to the confinement and isolation that limit women's mobility and their possibilities for fulfillment. Aguilar depicts women in enclosed patios; small, dark rooms; clandestine safe houses; and private chapels, all of which are spaces in which their movement is monitored and restricted. Furthermore, the women who venture from the confines of home fear danger outside these spaces, though the implicit threat varies from story to story. Whether or not the danger is imminent, Aguilar's women feel their vulnerability. Such a representation reveals the degree of psychological control exercised upon women in a male-centered culture that makes them objects of desire rather than subjects.

The women in Aguilar's stories must weigh the suffocation and psychological death they experience within the enclosure against the threat to life (social or physical) without. The result is a constant tension that remains unresolved in each of the works. Extensive focalized passages communicate disappointed expectations, anxiety, and frustrations; the frequent ellipses that punctuate these passages signal the hesitance of women to imagine and articulate longings that are prohibited. These narrative techniques reiterate the message of the plots: that there is no space for expression for many women within political and social structures configured to limit their potential. The ambiguous endings avoid closure in terms of plot, stressing not only the inconclusive nature of women's experiences, but also the structural impossibility of a satisfactory resolution.

Rosa Sarmiento: *Prehistory of a National Icon*

The story of Rosa Sarmiento and Rubén Darío provides Aguilar with an opportunity to explore the implications of women's marginalization and to dialogue with a textual tradition that seems to take that marginalization as a given. As Joan Scott notes in "The Problem of Invisibility," "The story of the development of human society has been told largely through male agency; and the identification of men with 'humanity' has resulted for the most part in the disappearance of women from the record of the past" (5). Nowhere is this more obvious, perhaps, than in the trajectory of the cultural development in Latin America, where this narrative is intimately linked to nation formation and the forging of a collective identity. Texts that contributed to the development of the "imagined community" of the nation have traditionally comprised the historical (and literary) canon. These cast historical events in epic terms of crises, triumph, and progress. In Nicaragua, the story of cultural achievement centers around the figure of Rubén Darío, modernist poet par excellence, frequently depicted as the gift of Nicaragua to the world of arts and letters.

In *Rosa Sarmiento* Aguilar appropriates a set of past events, namely the birth and early childhood of Darío, but she recasts them to reveal a plot strikingly different from that commonly detailed in both biographies and literary histories. Theorist and historian Hayden White has presented a number of critical premises that are particularly useful in understanding Aguilar's appropriation of history. According to White, the ideology of historiography is evident in the superimposition of different plot structures on past events. He writes that it is "in what appears to be the projection of a given generic plot type onto a given set of historical events, . . . that the question of the ideological nature of historical storytelling can be said to arise" ("Storytelling," 68). Though specifically addressing the question of the ideological bias of narrative itself, the comment posits an interesting variation on the idea that history is written by the victors. As Miguel León-Portilla's *Visión de los vencidos* (1959) demonstrates with regard to the Spanish Conquest, it is possible for peoples and cultures to discern entirely different plot structures in the same set of events. What was for Hernán Cortés a deftly maneuvered triumph gained by military strategy was for the Aztecs an epic defeat augured by portents and abetted by rulers and gods.

By retelling Darío's story in *Rosa Sarmiento,* Aguilar confronts the projection of the epic plot type onto the set of events surrounding the national hero Darío. Her version of the past engages the nationalist textual tradition about Darío in a way that emphasizes women's marginality and exclusion from the national plot. Rather than following the trajectory of Darío's life from childhood to international glory, Aguilar's novel centers on the world of Rosa Sarmiento, a woman who usually makes a brief entrance in biographies to give birth to the hero and then disappears.

Rosario Aguilar is not the first person to include Rubén Darío in the pages of literature. Indeed, Darío has long been a cultural icon in Nicaragua and an object of appropriation of groups from left to right. As Whisnant notes, when it comes to Darío, there are so many layers of interpretation and appropriation that contemporary critics may best approximate him if they view him as a cultural construct: "Darío in particular, because he never cast himself as an easily definable partisan figure, has been singled out as the repository of much of the country's most domestically and internationally negotiable cultural capital. . . . So protracted and convoluted has this process [of interpretation and appropriation] become that 'Rubén Darío' may now more usefully be understood as a political-cultural construct than as any identifiable historical personage" (440). The story of Darío's life is recounted in numerous biographies and in the oral traditions of Nicaragua, where school children have for years learned to recite his poetry and life story at an early age.

Many texts actively allegorize the story of Darío's life. Most biographies are constructed in epic terms, beginning with portents of the hero's birth and proceeding to early glimmers of genius in childhood, then concluding with his international success and untimely demise. They also mention Darío's desire for fame and acceptance by the elite of Europe, as well as his insecurity about the physical traits that belied an indigenous ancestry.

Like so many other biographies of nineteenth- and twentieth-century politicians and writers, Darío's becomes equated with the story of the nation. Biographical writers represent his life in a way that transcends the personal. This is not uncommon, according to Marchant: "In a move that equates personal experience with the life/history of the nation, the personal when marked as masculine is often seen to be representative in terms of the nation and therefore public. By contrast, the personal when marked as feminine is seen as private" (8). When the story of Darío is plotted according to a masculinist perspective, Rosa Sarmiento is a marginal figure, noticed only for her supporting role as biological mother. Her life supports no plot of progress and has no overtones of glory; her personal is private, not public.

While Rosa's personal trials are private, Darío's struggles represent the pretensions to grandeur of nineteenth-century Latin American states. Histories of literature consistently associate Darío's poetry and the modernist movement with the cultural coming of age of Latin America. His life—from troubled origins to international accolades—suggests to biographers the potential and promise of Latin America on the world scene. In contrast, *Rosa Sarmiento* intimates that modernism and nineteenth-century notions of progress did not necessarily have the same repercussions for women as they did for men. The question posed by feminists studying European history surfaces again. Just as they asked whether or not women had a Renaissance, Aguilar inquires about the extent of women's participation in the formation of Latin American cultural identity.

Like other texts, *Rosa Sarmiento* takes Darío's birth as the starting point for the story, though Aguilar chooses to focus on the mother and not the child. The overwhelming majority of Darío biographies begin with his birth, which is generally recounted in messianic terms, but they quickly move past prodigious events of his childhood to the publication of *Azul* in 1888. Aguilar instead lingers on the earlier years of Darío's life, in which his mother Rosa struggled with maternity and marital discontent, as well as her peripheral position in her extended family.

To show the overlooked life of Rosa Sarmiento, Aguilar recasts the same set of historical facts according to a different interpretative perspective. Her novel is thus fundamentally an intertextual work, informed by other biographies as well as Darío's own writings. However, it differs from these because in telling the story of Rosa, Aguilar does not plot events in epic terms.

From the inception of the novel, Aguilar makes clear both her dependence on tradition and her divergence from it. While most biographies delicately allude to the marital discontent of Rosa Sarmiento and her husband, Manuel García, Aguilar offers a different point of view. She confronts the difficulties of Rosa overtly, linking these not just to the lack of "moral character" of the husband but more especially to the precarious social position of the orphaned young woman dependent on her relatives. The first two pages of the novel mention "los parientes que quieren que se marche lejos" [the relatives who want her to go far away] and "quienes la quieren" [those who love her] (*Colección*, 1:145, 146). The remainder of the text gradually reveals the extent of their power over her.

In contrast, in the biography *Nacimiento y primera infancia de Rubén Darío* by Juan Vanegas and Alfonso Valle, the authors note that Manuel "parecía necesitar una compañera que controlara sus excesos y lo curara de la enfermedad de la política" (12) [seemed to need a wife who would control his excesses and cure him of the disease of politics]. The allusion to women as bastions of moral uprightness and good antidotes to politics stands out immediately, as does the insinuation that Rosa's husband was a less-than-perfect candidate for a prodigious union. Aguilar's text emphasizes the impossibility of Rosa serving as the moral guardian of her husband, exploding the myth that women economically, socially, and sexually subordinate might somehow reform the behavior of uncooperative spouses, even if the women were willing to take on such a role. Another biographer, Valentín de Pedro, puzzles that "no deja de resultar singularmente curioso, que el matrimonio se separe cuando está a punto de nacerles un hijo, lo que parece que debía contribuir a unirlos" (9) [it does not cease to be singularly curious that the marriage breaks apart just when a child is about to be born of the union, an event that, it seems, ought to have helped bring the couple together]. Aguilar elaborates at length on such speculations, beginning her novel with Rosa's thoughts as she awaits the arrival of the baby, intertwining her marital discontent with an overwhelming fear of maternity.

Rosa's pregnancy emphasizes even more her position as an object in society, steered toward conformity by the men and women of her adoptive family. However, her anxiety is about both maternity and motherhood, about the social and biological implications of having a child. Significantly, the novel suggests that both reduce her to an object at the mercy of forces she cannot control: "En su cuerpo alegre y esbelto, se han sucedido fenómenos tras fenómenos que han quebrado la armonía" (*Colección,* 1:145) [In her carefree, svelte body, change after change has occurred and broken the harmony]. Her desire is to flee, to escape the situation in which she finds herself: "Quiere huir, pero huir de la maternidad. . . . Quienes la quieren le han propuesto el viaje. Es una oportunidad para la que espera y teme. Para quien . . . ansía que los acontecimientos sucedan pronto, muy pronto. Salir de la encrucijada por cualquiera de sus caminos . . . y al mismo tiempo . . . que no suceda . . . arrepentirse, volverse en el tiempo y borrar el instante" (1:146) [She wants to flee, but flee from maternity. . . . Those who love her have proposed the trip. It is an opportunity for what she waits for and fears. For one . . . who longs for events to happen quickly, very quickly. To leave the crossroads by any of its paths ... and at the same time ... would that it not happen ... to repent, to go back in time and erase that moment]. The imperative and impossibility of escape recurs in the evocation of the female protagonists of Aguilar; they appear as the inevitable response to a repressive society and stifled will.

In the case of *Rosa Sarmiento,* the novel emphasizes the protagonist's dependence on her male protectors, namely her uncle and her spouse. As long as she carries this child or accepts the role of mother, she is subject to their authority. If she denies their authority, she loses her child; he is not hers and never has been because her sexuality and reproductive capacity do not belong to her. They are commodities to be guarded, regulated, and enjoyed by male authorities.

Aguilar highlights Rosa's position as object rather than subject of history in the scene of Rubén's baptism. In a passage focalized through Manuel, Rosa's estranged husband, the young woman appears as an object of desire: "Rosa ya no es la niña atolondrada con quien le han casado. Siente de pronto el deseo de volver a amarla. Es como que una mujer nueva ha surgido de ella ... y además, él tiene derecho (1:159) [Rosa is no longer the silly girl to whom they've married him. All of a sudden he feels the desire to love her again. It is as if a new women has arisen from her ... and besides, he has the right]. Here, the pleasure of the gaze is coupled with power; Manuel desires and has the power to act upon desire. The male gaze again converts the female into an object he wishes to possess: "Don Manuel, por verla, casi no ha visto a su propio hijo. Ella está radiante" (1:159) [Don Manuel has hardly seen his own son, for all his looking at her. She [Rosa] is radiant]. In the lines that follow, Aguilar continues to show the young woman through the male gaze, a sharp contrast to the rest of the text, where the passages are focalized through Rosa, who appears as a human subject in search of happiness, affirmation, and freedom.

As the novel depicts Rosa's frustrated search for fulfillment, it becomes increasingly obvious that she moves in a world with a rhythm different from that of her family. She does not participate in the epic plot of Darío's life. She does not apprehend any of the significance bestowed upon her by later writers. Aguilar makes reference to this frequently, employing phrases such as "ella no lo sabe" (1:146) [she does not know it], "no sospecha Rosa" (1:147) [Rosa doesn't suspect], "no presiente Rosa" (1:148) [Rosa does not sense]. Such phrases emphasize the constructedness of Darío's biography, as well as Rosa's unawareness of her role in their grandiose plots.

After the birth of the child, Rosa definitively passes to a peripheral position in the family. Frustrated and alone, she subsequently rebels against the confinement of the house she shares with Manuel. She rejects both the protection of matrimony and the solace of religion, the two options pushed upon her by the women of the family: "No puede ser como las otras mujeres de la familia que se resignan prematuramente a la resignación. La vida se les pasa viendo crecer a los hijos, rezando, sin saber nunca lo que hay dentro de ellas mismas y que sin conocerlo se marchita. . . . Las mujeres de su época permanecen en sus casas, silenciosas, con las cabezas sumisas y sin rebelarse jamás. Biológicamente viviendo, pariendo hijos sin saber cómo ni para qué" (1:167) [She cannot be like the other women of the family, who resign themselves prematurely to being resigned. Life passes them by as they watch their children grow, praying, never knowing what there is inside them, and without knowing it, it withers away. The women of her time stay in their houses, silent, with heads bowed, never rebelling. Living biologically, birthing children without knowing how or why]. What is particularly interesting in this focalized passage is the depiction of maternity and motherhood as possibilities that can be disliked or rejected by women. Maternity and motherhood are identified with the submissiveness and subjugation prescribed by church and state. The passage emphasizes the psychological repercussions of the *encierro* (confinement) and ensilio of women in a culture that mythologizes and idealizes their position as mothers but denies them any space for the realization of their desires. There is no room for fulfillment within the confines of motherhood as it is constructed in Rosa's culture, and its rejection means ostracism as well, as Aguilar emphasizes in the novel's conclusion.

The last pages of the novel show Rosa's definitive divorce from the glory of Rubén Darío. Having opted for personal satisfaction in the form of an illicit union with another man, she is separated from her child. The last lines of the novel reveal the implications of the decision Rosa has made: "La puerta de la casa se ha cerrado al empujarla el viento. Al llegar, siente la necesidad de recostarse contra la pared, siente un inmenso peso sobre su cuerpo . . . una densa y extraña obscuridad que la envuelve, que la aísla y la deja fuera para siempre . . ." (1:180; ellipses in original) [The wind has pushed the door of the house shut. When she arrives, she feels the need to rest against the wall, feels an enormous weight upon her body . . . a dense and strange darkness that envelops her, that isolates her and leaves her out forever]. According to this representation, Rosa appears as the object of forces that determine her fate. The sentence structure makes clear that she does not act, but rather is acted upon by something larger than herself. Even the door is shut on her by the wind. As in other novels, the net effect of these events is the isolation and estrangement of the female protagonist from society, in this case, the grandiose success of Latin America's poet laureate Rubén Darío.

Las Doce y Veintinueve: *The (De)Construction of Small Worlds*

Like *Rosa Sarmiento*, *Las doce y veintinueve* appropriates a particularly dramatic moment in Nicaraguan history, exploring Nicaraguan society at the moment of the 1972 earthquake that shook Managua. The novel is an example of novelistic polyphony in Bakhtinian terms, though it is interesting to note that as in *Rosa*, the underlying insistence of the narrative is on the isolation of the individuals and their inability to communicate and interact. While historiographic and journalistic representations emphasize the political repercussions of the earthquake and the immense human tragedy, Aguilar's novel relates the tragedy as it acts upon the life of one person. In telling the story of Vilma, a young, upper-class mother of two, Aguilar constructs a cross-section of Nicaraguan life at the moment of the 1972 temblor. In ever-expanding circles of social interaction, she incorporates more individuals and voices: Vilma; Vilma's husband, Manuel; Manuel's lover; the family maid; the maid's *compañero;* the maid's former employers; and so on. This particular sort of heteroglossia is common in Aguilar's historical writing, in whose plots an individual's life story is implicated in ever-larger spheres of human relationships. As in other stories, the polyphony gives shape to a singularly devastating event (such as conquest or revolution) and also highlights social and economic injustices prevalent within the region.

The image that emerges from *Las doce y veintinueve* is of a family in ruins and a nation absolutely devastated not only by the earthquake but also by an underlying structure of inequity and injustice. Although the present of the text is the time immediately preceding and following the 1972 earthquake, the focalized analepses take the text beyond 1972 to broaden the temporal scope of the novel. These flashbacks present personal histories of rural-urban migration, internal colonization, political injustice, and sexual and racial hierarchies in Nicaragua. As the polyphonic narrative moves around the figure of Vilma, it uncovers often invisible social problems, including domestic abuse, racism, snobbery, and the persistence of violence and political corruption.

As in other texts by Rosario Aguilar, the narrative technique of focalization plays a particularly important role in *Las doce y veintinueve.* In this case, the frequent depiction of the interior worlds of the protagonists emphasizes their isolation and inability to communicate. The differences between Vilma and Manuel's interior worlds reveal glaring contrasts in the social options of men and women, and other passages highlight their family's isolation from the troubling social reality that exists in Nicaragua.

Various textual clues indicate that problems plague the relationship between Vilma and her husband, but it is the focalization that reveals the degree of separation brought about by their unquestioning assumption of the traditional roles society offers them. The passages focalized through Vilma underscore the lingering questions about the future of the couple. They also reveal Vilma's distance from her husband and his world of business and an extramarital affair. At the beginning of the novel, a focalized passage expresses Vilma's doubts about her marriage: "Estaba llegando al convencimiento, en aquel preciso instante, de que su matrimonio fracasaba, se hundía sin remedio aparente. . . . Si todo fracasaba . . . ¿Qúe hacer?" (1:66) [She was coming to the conclusion, at that precise moment, that her marriage was a failure, that it was sinking without any apparent remedy. . . . If everything fell apart. . . . What to do?] The text presents the boredom of the upper-class woman, her internalization of feelings of blame and guilt, and the limited options available to her. The only alternative to marriage that she has is a return to her hometown, and she opts for a short-term solution by taking pills for her nerves.

For Manuel, Vilma is a necessary fixture in his world, in part because she lends meaning to his existence and assures his good standing in society. This is especially obvious in a passage in which he ponders his own infidelity to her: "Y, ¿si ella decide dejarlo y se lleva a los niños? No, no los dejará irse por nada del mundo, porque si eso sucede sería para él casi como una sentencia de muerte. Inmediatamente su mundo se derrumbaría. Todo ese mundo construido por él mismo para que en él vivan Vilma y sus hijos" (1:76) [And if she decides to leave him and she takes the children? No, no he will not let them go for anything in the world because if that happens, it would be like a death sentence for him. His world would immediately collapse. That whole world he himself has built so that Vilma and his children may live in it]. Vilma is necessary to preserve his self-image; he professes to be unable to live without her because she justifies the existence of "todo ese mundo construido."

Interestingly enough, as Ann González notes, the quake momentarily restores the social order in the family and the nation. In the novel, tragedy pushes both individuals and the Somoza regime to their logical extremes. The guards protect private property, shooting anyone associated with looters while the guards themselves steal for personal gain at the expense of the devastated nation. In actuality in Nicaragua, law and order disintegrated during three days of looting by National Guard troops, and Somoza established the National Emergency Committee, which allowed him eventually to misuse relief funds and regain control of the government (Bulmer-Thomas, 257). In Vilma and Manuel's household, Manuel returns to his house and family to reassert control, using violence to impose order.

The scene of Manuel's return is particularly significant because of the way in which it presents Vilma's reaction when Manuel appears in front of the ruins of the house: "La mujer se le lanza encima, pero no para abrazarlo, no. . . . Con los puños cerrados le golpea y le grita cosas incomprensibles, terribles, jamás antes moduladas por su boca. Palabras en las que parece acusarlo de que, por el hecho de estar ausente, lejos de ellos, todo el mundo ha perecido. Como si quisiera culparle, por todo lo que está sucediéndo en el mundo, su destrucción, su hundimiento" (1:83) [The woman hurls herself on him, but not to embrace him, no. . . . With closed fists she beats him and screams at him incomprehensible, terrible things never before uttered by her mouth. Words in which she appears to accuse him, to say that because he has been absent, far from them, that the whole world has perished. As if she wanted to blame him for everything that is happening in the world, for its destruction, its ruin]. Vilma's only sphere of action has been within the family, the symbol of which was their home. When this is absolutely devastated, she reacts with violence against Manuel, who had provided her with the house that was at once refuge and prison. The reaction is telling; Vilma recognizes that her husband is responsible for the construction of her peaceful world, and she blames his marital failures for the crumbling of it.

For Manuel, the destruction creates an escape from his involvement with the young woman from the Atlantic coast, and he restores his position of power in the family by force. Hence, the apparent resolution to the story: the absent and unfaithful husband returns, the wife acquiesces after he strikes her, and the family leaves town. Manuel reclaims his place as the head of the family unit, and Vilma resumes the role of wife and mother. However, Aguilar implies that the family, like the nation, has been rent too deeply to be so easily "healed" and that a restoration of order does not imply that old grievances have been addressed.

Images of desolation permeate the text, and fissures at all social levels become visible. Vilma and Manuel are isolated in their own worlds, and the biological bridge between them, "el baby," perishes in the quake. Additionally, the distinction between public and private is quite literally destroyed, leaving each to negotiate reality on his or her own terms. Vilma is lost in a world that is suddenly too big, the poor take advantage of chaos to seek material goods they have always lacked, and the National Guard uses the moment to assert supremacy and enrich their ranks.

In showing the collapse of the country and the reassertion of control by powerful males (Manuel, the Guard), the novel interrogates the nature of the social system in place and points to the latent resistance beneath the surface. The world that collapsed was constructed to protect the integrity of male property (sexual, material, political) at the level of the family and the nation. The brute force employed in the reimposition of this system uncovers the violence that long existed beneath the surface of society. No facile resolution exists in *Las doce y veintinueve,* and there is an implication of future rupture in both family and nation. As Vilma returns to her parents' home, she wonders if she and Manuel will ever repair their relationship. In terms of the nation, it is possible to see clearly the seeds of rebellion sown in the days following the quake.

Women and Revolution: Intimate-National Conflicts

The growing resistance to political oppression erupted in Nicaraguan society in the revolutionary movements that eventually toppled the Somoza dictatorship. Aguilar's novels of the Nicaraguan revolution emphasize women's actions as citizens, "a position that had been difficult for them to assume as long as the public sphere was assumed to be a masculine domain" (Franco, "Going Public," 66). As Franco and others have noted, the state-sponsored violence of the 1970s in Latin America produced a radical change in society that affected not only the political but also the gender order. The stories of *El guerrillero* and *Siete relatos* concern women during a particularly traumatic period of Nicaraguan history, namely the period of guerrilla activity, revolution, and counterrevolution. During this time the distinctions maintained between private and public were questioned, and Aguilar's novels show the effects wrought by these changes in women's lives.

As in other texts by Aguilar, the narrative polyphony of the two novels is again readily apparent. Both *El guerrillero* and *Siete relatos* are narratively complex, incorporating focalization, analepsis, and numerous intertextual references to relate the story of the revolution. The polyphony of the texts constructs a world that describes the diversity of Nicaraguan cultures at that particular moment, while the recurrence to focalization insists on personal interpretations of reality and denies any authoritative account of the revolution. Furthermore, these techniques fictionalize history in such a way as to recast the tumultuous events of the past through individual women's experiences. Aguilar thus incorporates into the texts multiple interpretations of revolution, family structure, economic realities, and social obligations.

El guerrillero, for instance, offers a view of revolutionary activity through the life of an arguably apolitical individual, the rural primary school teacher who is the protagonist. It also probes the human repercussions of economic hardship, women's sexual inequality, and political violence. I am especially concerned here with Aguilar's incorporation of other texts into the novel, a technique that widens the scope of the story and locates the struggle of the female protagonist within a larger cultural context of national politics, the Latin American Left, and revolutionary struggle.

The intertextuality of *El guerrillero,* coupled with the frequent focalization through the protagonist, demonstrates the effects of women's discursive entry into the national culture. The narrative frequently shows the interpenetration of national discourse in the thoughts of the teacher, as well as her adaptation of this rhetoric according to her personal circumstances. Her access to public discourse is a product of nineteenth-century liberal programs of public education, initiated to consolidate national identity and promote progress. However, the teacher manipulates these programs according to her present reality of economic injustice and revolutionary activity. As she claims that discourse for her own ends, the teacher questions the ideological underpinnings of the nation and the policies that defend it.

The appropriation of texts by the teacher in *El guerrillero* represents a significant instance of intertextuality, especially since the majority of the references are to schoolbooks and Latin American poetry. Aguilar's representation of one woman's manipulation of language reveals the processes by which people receive and engage the rhetoric of the state. As Bakhtin points out, "For any individual consciousness living in it, language is not an abstract system of normative forms but rather a concrete heteroglot conception of the world" (293). *El guerrillero* shows what happens when particular women take hold of this conception of the world and place themselves into it by speaking and writing. Aguilar's fictionalization of Central America's recent past thus dramatizes women's increasing appropriation of the symbolic currency of the nation. As Lerner intuits in the epigraph to this chapter, as women make a space for their own speaking and acting, they change the configuration of the entire system. Again, Bakhtin states, "Consciousness finds itself inevitably facing the necessity of *having to choose a language.* With each literary-verbal performance, consciousness must actively orient itself amidst heteroglossia, it must move in and occupy a position for itself within it, it chooses, in other words, a 'language'" (295; emphasis in original). In this case, the discourse the novel incorporates is important because it signals the erasure of lines between public and private. It also reveals the politicization of personal life. Aguilar shows the increasing penetration of the public discourse of the nation in the private world of the teacher, but she also emphasizes that the teacher is not a passive recipient and transmitter of the education and messages of the state. Rather, as the teacher's personal life becomes intermingled with the public discourse and national conflict, she becomes more active in public events and more assertive in pursuit of her desires.

The incorporation of the language of schoolbooks into the text shows the woman's interaction with one of the principal tools mobilized in the establishment of national identity. The rural teacher takes the lessons in mathematics, national history, and geography as a palimpsest upon which she inscribes her own story, emotions, and experiences. Explanations of mathematical problems, geography, and climate become transformed in focalized passages in the text where the teacher inserts her daily reality into the narrative of the curriculum.

This incorporation and manipulation of pedagogical discourse in a woman-centered novel is significant, especially in light of Jean Franco's observation of the importance of pedagogical discourse in the legitimation of the state. In "The Nation as Imagined Community," Franco discusses the exposure of state legitimation in a passage from *El otoño del patriarca* (1975) by Gabriel García Márquez. She emphasizes that in García Márquez's novel certain passages "expose the way the nation state is legitimized through pedagogical discourse—for example, the geography text book" (206). In a similar way, Aguilar reveals the constructedness of pedagogical discourse, as well as its distance from the physical and psychological realities of the state's inhabitants.

The insertion of the rural teacher in the subject position of these texts reconfigures discourse on science, geography, and math. Her reinterpretation of seemingly innocuous, objective texts reveals the "fictional" (constructed) nature of the world that they propose and offers a counterimagination of the state. Consider, for example, this passage, in which a basic geography lesson is changed to incorporate the reality of armed struggle, fear, and maternity:

> el clima de Nicaragua es cálido, pero fresco en las sierras. Las esta-ciones de Nicaragua son: invierno o época de lluvias y verano o época seca. Ay, amor, mejor no te hubieras ido por esos caminos que deben estar llenos de lodo. . . . Los productos principales son: café, a lo mejor te fuiste para el lado de las sierras, a los campamentos de café, allí tu lucecita confundida entre las lucecitas de los hachones. . . . En Nicaragua hay minas de oro y plata. Adentro de mí, tu hijo, hondo, muy hondo, como las minas. Estoy triste, el muchachito nacerá triste. De las minas de Nicaragua sólo se extraen tristezas (3:46–47) [The climate of Nicaragua is hot, but cool in the mountains. The seasons of Nicaragua are winter, or rainy season, and summer, or dry season. Oh, my love, it would have been better if you'd not gone on those roads that likely are full of mud. . . . The principal products are coffee, you probably went to the mountains, to the coffee fields, there is your tiny light lost amid the lights of the torches. . . . In Nicaragua, there are gold and silver mines. Your child, deep within me, very deep like the mines. I am sad, the little one will be born sad. From the mines of Nicaragua, only sorrows are extracted].

In this passage, Aguilar combines the languages of nationalist primary school texts, social revolution, and a consciousness of maternity. Similar passages interspersed throughout text serve to emphasize the distance of this woman from the material she teaches. They also disclose the social reality that demands that these lessons be subverted.

Not only passages from school texts but also fragments from Pablo Neruda's poetry surface in the pages of the novel. The repetition by the protagonist of a line from one of Neruda's love poems affects a subtle change in the interpretation of the poem in that it locates the woman in the position of the lover rather than the beloved. The teacher's refrain throughout the story is "cómo no haber amado sus grandes ojos fijos" [how could one not have loved his large, steady eyes].[2] In taking hold of this line to explain her relationship with the guerrillero, she locates herself in the subject position of desiring. It is her gaze that admires the captivating "ojos fijos."

The intertextuality and the spatial configurations of this novel reveal both the possibilities and the limitations of women's participation in the cultural and social life of the nation. As Higonnet notes, the analysis of space is a concern for those interested in gender studies, particularly feminists: "Feminist literary critics have begun to . . . trace the ways writers inscribe gender onto the symbolic representations of space within texts, whether through images of physical confinement, of exile and exclusions, of property and territoriality, or of the body as the interface between individual and communal identities" ("New Cartographies," 2). Aguilar's works highlight the spatial limitations imposed upon women, connecting the restrictions to the women's feelings of confinement, isolation, and discontent. As discussed earlier, her works show a heightened awareness of the female body as the "interface between individual and communal identities," especially with regard to maternity.

Aguilar frequently depicts women rebelling against the small enclosures to which they have been relegated. In *El guerrillero*, the teacher moves in small spaces: her house, the hiding place of the revolutionary fighter, the classroom. When the text depicts her activities outside these spaces, her movement is insistently associated with her fear of reprisals against her life. In two instances, Aguilar shows the protagonist far beyond the village, once when she seeks an illegal abortion and again when she attempts to identify the bodies of fallen revolutionaries. Her fear in open spaces suggests a culture that has prescribed confinement for women and visits violence upon their persons if they trespass its borders.

The anguish of the teacher's decision to seek an abortion emphasizes both the moral dilemma she faces and the political nature of her sexuality. In this way, Aguilar's story gives literary representation not only to the abortion issue but also to the underlying abuse suffered by many Latin American women. The teacher finds herself pregnant after acquiescing to the coercion of a local judge, who pursues an exploitative and implicitly violent sexual relationship with her. She resolves to end the pregnancy because she sees this as the only way to maintain her independence and sever the relationship.

As in the story of the young woman from the Atlantic coast in *Las doce y veintinueve, El guerrillero* points to the commodification of women's sexuality in a patriarchal culture predicated upon women's inferior social and economic position. Here it is useful to cite Lerner's observation in *Creation of Patriarchy:* "Since their sexuality, an aspect of their body, was controlled by others, women were not only actually disadvantaged but psychologically restrained in a very special way. For women, as for men of subordinate and oppressed groups, history consisted of their struggle for emancipation and freedom from necessity. But women struggled against different forms of oppression and domination than did men" (214).

Aguilar's novels of the revolution very effectively integrate a representation of the "different forms of oppression and domination" against which women struggle, locating the search for their emancipation within a context of generalized turmoil. Though women's struggle is generally depicted as a personal one for individual rights, Aguilar shows that it is a political challenge as well. For instance, after finding out she is pregnant by the judge, the teacher is faced with the impossibility of seeking advice or help, the difficulty of raising her first child in poverty, and her reluctance to end the pregnancy for moral or ethical reasons. The promise she makes to herself while having the abortion seals her political commitment: "Promete entregarse de lleno a aquella fila interminable de rostros infinitos de niños. . . . Repartir todo lo que como madre es capaz de dar y hacer por un hijo" (3:77) [She promises to dedicate herself fully to that interminable line of endless faces of children. To give everything that as a mother she is capable of giving and doing for a child]. In this way, the maternal question is transposed to another level, and the teacher resolves her personal moral dilemma by making a promise at once political and personal: to do all in her power to secure the well-being of her pupils.

The conclusion of the novel finds the woman surrounded by her pupils, engaged in a soliloquy that is part school text, part benediction and call to resistance. As she bids farewell to her infatuation with the guerrillero, she affirms her commitment to continued resistance, ending with the words, "no te dejés atrapar. . . . no te dejés atrapar, amor" (3:104) [don't let yourself get caught. . . . don't let yourself get caught, my love]. This particular fictionalization of Central American history, then, shows the psychological and political maturation of a female protagonist who, coincidentally, resurfaces in *Siete relatos* in a much more radical role.

Like *El guerrillero, Siete relatos sobre el amor y la guerra* is a fictionalized account of the revolutionary years in Nicaragua, incorporating images of the revolution before and after its triumph. However, the novel is unique because it is fundamentally decentralized; it reveals various sides of the revolutionary regime by presenting multiple female protagonists. The women are martyrs, exiles, literacy volunteers, and bureaucrats from all social classes. Though the novel has no clear protagonist, the revolution is the common denominator for each of the stories of the women whose lives are affected by the struggle.

The *siete relatos* of the title are the stories of seven different women. The title significantly links the idea of love, associated with private life, and war, a political phenomenon, though the entirety of the text deconstructs this binary through the vignettes about women's experiences in love and war. The first part of the book, "Sobre el amor," concerns three women whose lives are strangely intertwined by the revolution and their amorous relationships. Leticia lives in the Atlantic coast region with her possessive Miskito spouse, while her sister, Paula, has an affair with Eddy. Eddy, in turn, is María Elena's attractive, bourgeois husband who jets between Miami and Managua to lobby on behalf of his family in hopes of recovering their confiscated property. In the segment supposedly "On love," the disappointments of the three women dominate the stories. Each finds herself alone and isolated, whether in exile or not.

The second part of the book, "Sobre la guerra" (On war), presents María José, Margarita (alias Karla, the teacher from *El guerrillero*), Lucía, and Sonia, four young revolutionaries inextricably caught in the fight for national liberation. This fictionalization of Nicaragua's past portrays women's active participation in the revolution, in this case in the final offensive in León. Again, it shows the inseparability of political and gender issues. More linear than the first part of the book, the stories form a bricolage of images that culminate on July 19, 1979, with the victory celebration in Managua.[3] Despite the optimistic conclusion, it is impossible to disregard the earlier portion of the book, which insists that social injustice, especially in the arena of gender relations, persisted in the years of the revolutionary regime.

What are the implications of such a decentralized, polyphonic novel about "love and war"? The text not only provides a vision of the revolution different from testimonials and memoirs, it also participates in what Nelly Richard posits as a vital process for cultural criticism. Richard sees selection, recombination, and resemantization as essential operations for "cualquier operatoria textual (femenina o latinoamericana) que se enfrenta al sistema presuntamente clausurado ... de las categorizaciones hegemónicas que simbolizan la autoridad del Todo como metáfora del saber universal" (25) [any textual operation (feminine or Latin American) that confronts a supposedly closed system ... of hegemonic categories that symbolize the authority of the Whole as a metaphor for universal knowledge]. In Nicaragua, the revolution in many ways became a "Todo" to explain, justify, and control, increasingly so as the nation suffered under the U.S. embargo and threats of military intervention. It is possible to see a critical response to revolutionary authority in the texts of both Gioconda Belli and Rosario Aguilar. Both authors were sympathetic to the revolutionary ideals but also especially aware of the persistence of inequities in gender relations during and after the Sandinista period in Nicaragua. In Aguilar there is a tendency toward a fragmented, decentralized discourse that stymies any fixed interpretation of the cultural referent, whether that is the revolution, Conquest, or the life of Rubén Darío. It is seen most obviously in *Siete relatos,* which multiplies interpretations of the revolution and of women's experiences in that culture.

Though Aguilar depicts women in various circumstances, it is significant that she highlights their actual or perceived entrapment in all but the last vignette on Margarita, alias Karla. The feeling of psychological confinement associated with maternity surfaces several times, especially in the stories of María Elena, Leticia, and María José. Each laments the fact that her biological state as expectant mother limits her mobility and impedes her desires. This frustration is exacerbated by the fact that none can rely on a sympathetic partner with whom she shares an egalitarian relationship. María Elena, for instance, finds that her pregnancy will keep her from accompanying her husband to Nicaragua: "yo había quedado embarazada y todos estaban felices, menos yo ... porque era obvio que en mi estado un poco delicado no podía viajar. Volver" (54) [I had gotten pregnant and everyone was happy but me ... because it was obvious that in my rather delicate state that I could not travel. Return]. Under the watchful eye of her wealthy in-laws, María Elena remains in Miami while her husband Eddy has an affair in Nicaragua with Paula, who also becomes pregnant. Paula's sister Leticia similarly finds herself isolated and trapped far from the city, since her possessive husband will not permit her to leave the Atlantic coast with "his" child: "La mujer va sustituyendo cada pedacito de amor que siente por el hombre por una especie de rancor. . . . Porque se ha vuelto una prisionera de sus bellos colores. No, no puede quedarse allí, enterrada en vida. . . . Si ella lograra huir, Cristy la perseguiría por todos los caminos. . . . ¿Qué no haría para encontrar a su hijo?" (86) [The woman takes each little piece of love that she feels for the man and substitutes it with a kind of resentment. Because she has become a prisoner of his beautiful colors. No, she cannot stay here, buried alive. . . . If she manages to flee, Cristy will follow her by all roads. . . . What wouldn't he do to find his son?]. In each of these stories, Aguilar again reveals women's bodies as an "interface between individual and communal identities," and probes the physical and psychological repercussions of this reality for women.

Aguilar also frequently shows women limited by their economic and psychological dependence on men in her novels. In *Siete relatos* various protagonists come to terms with their lack of autonomy as they begin to take action in society and politics. For instance, María Elena becomes involved with a Cuban exile, takes a job, requests political asylum, and confronts her husband with a request for divorce. Though she is astutely aware of the limitations placed upon her in the new world of North American capitalism, María Elena takes the benefits it affords her in order to negotiate a space for herself in the world of exile: "[E]sas personas tan sólo piensan en el negocio, no les interesan mis problemas personales ni mi status migratorio. . . . Me valorarán de una sola ojeada, de un solo golpe; mi figura, mi personalidad, mis atributos. Si sirven o no para demostrar los productos. Nada más" (34) [Those people only think about business, they're not interested in my personal problems or my immigration status. . . . They evaluate me in a single glance, all at once; my figure, my personality, my attributes. If they are useful or not, to show off their products. Nothing more]. Though in an entirely different political context, Paula takes much the same action. She finally gives up on Eddy and asks her supervisor at work for help in getting medical attention for her sick child. Lerner offers an explanation that can account for the attraction of Eddy for both María Elena and Paula: "It was a rational choice for women, under conditions of powerlessness and economic dependency, to choose strong protectors for themselves and their children" (*Creation*, 218). Eddy is perceived as a "strong protector" because he has all the physical trappings of such a person; he is athletic and rich, with a fair complexion and upper-class background. Other men are also coded as protectors: the virile Cristy in *Siete relatos* and the faithful sergeant in *El guerrillero*. In the particular historical context of revolution, Aguilar's fictions explore the possibilities for women who turn from these strong protectors. In particular, Aguilar depicts the continued limitations on women's freedom and also the spaces they create for the pursuit of their own desires.

The story of Margarita represents Aguilar's most complete elaboration of the process of coming to consciousness in political and personal terms. Margarita Maradiaga, alias Karla, is the rural schoolteacher from *El guerrillero*. She resurfaces in *Siete relatos* as a member of the revolutionary organization responsible for securing safe houses for clandestine members of the struggle. After surviving the last days of violence before the triumph, she takes her child to Managua to witness the victory celebration and there spots her former guerrillero lover in the crowd. Through this scene, Aguilar proposes a significant resolution that binds together many of the different issues that have appeared in the narrative. In seeing the guerrillero again, Margarita confronts her own romantic notions of love and war, takes pride in her contribution to the victory, and anticipates her continued participation in the life of the nation: "Se dio cuenta de que lo que más deseaba . . . eran tan sólo un hogar para criar a su hijo. Paz para poder preparar, concienzudamente, los programas escolares. Enseñar. . . . Desde ese mismo instante dejó de ser 'Karla.' Recobró su legítima identidad. Margarita Maradiaga. Maestra rural" (154) [She realized that what she wanted most . . . was simply a home in which to raise her child. Peace to be able to prepare lesson plans conscientiously. To teach. . . . From that moment on she ceased to be "Karla." She recovered her legitimate identity. Margarita Maradiaga. Rural schoolteacher]. These last lines of the novel reveal the complete dissolution of the distinction between the public and private endeavors and associate Margarita's recuperation of her identity with the realization of her purpose in society as both a mother and teacher.

The Colony and the Present:
La niña blanca y los pájaros sin pies

Though it is relatively easy to offer fictionalized histories of the recent past, the task of inserting women into the colonial and national past is a difficult undertaking. However, it has proven attractive to numerous Central American women writers, most notably Gioconda Belli and Tatiana Lobo. Aguilar offers a twist in *La niña blanca y los pájaros sin pies,* a metafictional text about one woman's desire to conjure up her predecessors in a novel.

Responding to a comment by Stephen Greenblatt in which he cited the "desire to speak with the dead" as an origin of his New Historicist practice, Helen Buss observed, "Feminist scholars interested in finding the silenced voices of history and literature cannot begin merely with an effort to speak with the famous 'dead' of men's historical and literary traditions. We hardly know who our dead are" (86). In her own studies of women's history in literature, Buss examines women's private writing to approximate "women's cultural and personal development" (86). However, there are few such examples from colonial Latin America, with the notable exception of nuns' texts, such as those studied by Electa Arenal and Stacey Schlau (1989).

In the absence of a corpus of private writing by colonial women, Aguilar recurs to another strategy of historical recuperation. Like

Tatiana Lobo would do in *Entre Dios y el Diablo,* she imagines their experiences through an interrogation of male-authored texts. In *La niña blanca,* Aguilar creates an author-protagonist who moves from the same premise as feminist scholar Joan Scott, that women have not been "inactive or absent from events that made history, but that they have systematically been left out of the official record" (5). Scott has noted that "in the evaluation of what is important, women as individuals or as a definable group rarely receive mention" (5). This is certainly the case in colonial Latin America, where the story of the Spanish Conquest is that of the conquerors, and little mention is made of the women that peopled the world they left and the continent they sought to dominate. Imagining the other side of the events that changed the world, as Aguilar does in *La niña blanca,* alters our perception of history and provides background for modern political and social developments.

The metafictional nature of *La niña blanca* makes it a unique text in Central American women's literature produced in the late twentieth century. It is a text that participates fully in the contemporary discourse of transnational politics, globalization, and Latin American cultural identity. The protagonist is a woman writing about women. She is prompted to think of the past by a visit she makes to León Viejo with a Spanish reporter who comes to Nicaragua to cover the elections.[4] The protagonist's imaginations of women's reality during the years of conquest comprise chapters that carry the names of famous women from that period. These segments alternate with chapters in the voice of the protagonist as she writes about her experiences and the writing process.

The presentation of the colonial past in a metafictional text creates an alternative vision of colonial personalities through their incorporation into a different plot. As Bakhtin has noted, "New images in literature are very often created through a re-accentuating of old images, by translating them from one accentual register to another" (421). In *La niña blanca,* the technique at once presents new images of the colonial past and points to the fictionality of these renderings. The novel takes the tropes of the conqueror and barbarian from colonial texts and reworks them in a metafictional novel that straddles Nicaragua's colonial past and democratic transition in 1990.

The protagonist-author draws comparisons and contrasts between the reality in which she moves and the world of her own protagonists, linking together two moments of rupture in Central American society. Numerous references compare the Spanish reporter she meets during the electoral campaign with the Spanish scribes of the Conquest; "Era todo un cronista, español" [He was every bit the chronicler, Spanish] and "me contrató como su asistente y guía" (43) [he hired me as his assistant and guide] are the two phrases which introduce him in the text. Like his predecessors, the reporter comes to the Americas, gathers information on behalf of European superiors, and takes on a local woman to serve as guide. Like her American antecedents, the woman accompanies him on journeys throughout Central America. There the similarities end, for in this fictional world it is the woman who tells the story.

The dispute between the reporter and the Nicaraguan protagonist-author over the sort of characters the novel should include is a metafictional moment of some import. The protagonist-author remarks that she had written two chapters: "Cada uno se sostenía por sí solo y podía constituir una historia separada, pero yo quería que estuvieran unidos en una sola" (84) [Each one stood alone and could constitute a separate story, but I wanted them to come together in a single narrative]. When her Spanish companion suggests an indigenous protagonist with a mortal hatred of the Spanish, she responds that she cannot find a satisfactory one "en los libros de historia, en las calles" (84) [in the history books, in the streets]. She continues, noting that perhaps she cannot envision such a protagonist "porque la habían sometido ... [o] había pasado tanto tiempo que había sido borrada su huella" (84) [because she has been subjugated ... [or] because so much time has passed that her traces have been erased]. The awareness of the erasure of women's presence is common throughout the works of Rosario Aguilar and other Central American writers interested in the history of women. The author-protagonist's statement is an acknowledgment of reality and of the frustration it presents for women who want to produce a coherent history of their antecedents.

Within the colonial-era vignettes supposedly penned by the protagonist, the technique Aguilar adopts to approximate women's fragmented history is similar to that of Lobo's *Asalto al paraíso,* published in the same year in Costa Rica. Lobo presents an indigenous woman who cannot speak, making use of an auditory metaphor that emphasizes silence and muteness. In *La niña blanca,* a visual rather than an auditory metaphor pervades the text. Words like *silueta* (silhouette) and *perfil* (profile) are used frequently in the stories and suggest not only the incomprehensibility of the American continent for the colonizing Europeans but also the inability of modern writers to access a detailed vision of the past. What remain from the colonial past are only silhouettes, outlines, and shells of lives and structures, which fascinate Aguilar's contemporary protagonist. *La niña blanca* is the story of their reconstruction in fiction.

The episodes about colonial Central American women—Isabel, Luisa, Beatriz, María—signal the difficulties of colonial women, including indigenous, mestiza, and Spanish women. The chapters center not on physical challenges but rather on the isolation, frustration, and sense of powerlessness that each woman encountered and against which some rebelled. Whether Spanish or Indian, wives, mistresses, or daughters, according to Aguilar's presentation, each woman suffered the subordination of her own desires in the patriarchal world that defined her role. For instance, Isabel is portrayed as the reluctant defender of her husband, Pedrarias. Aguilar evokes her predicament as she is caught between her personal loathing of her husband, the accusations of his enemies, and the mistrust her own daughters have of her. Because of the patriarchal social structure of imperial Spain, Isabel has no choice but to stand by Pedrarias in order to protect her daughters, for whom she may procure suitable marriages only with the wealth her husband has acquired through brutality in the Indies. Her complicity, however, comes at a high cost; it leaves her unable to act on her own conscience with impunity and causes a breach between her and her daughters.

Similarly, Luisa, the indigenous noblewoman who is the subject of the second colonial vignette, has an extremely limited sphere of action. Unlike Isabel, though, Luisa is trapped by the competing demands of two patriarchal systems, the indigenous and the Spanish. In Aguilar's story, Luisa's body is depicted as the site of inscription of masculinist desires of conquest and dominance by both groups. The growing tensions between the cultures push the woman from privilege to subalternity in a matter of a few years.

A figure much like La Malinche in the Mexican Conquest, Luisa is given to Pedro de Alvarado as a wife, but she is quickly relegated to the status of a concubine after the tumult of conquest. Throughout the section on Luisa, Aguilar employs both focalization and the passive voice; the former communicates Luisa's interior world, while the latter emphasizes her object status, even within her own thoughts. Consider, for example, the following passage: "Así que quede constancia y resumido: fui escogida junto a otras cuatro doncellas como una estrategia de guerra. Un pacto entre los caciques y los poderosos señores extranjeros. Me toca esa suerte por ser noble y virgen. . . . Mi padre me ha destinado para esposa del Gran Señor. . . . Y yo he consentido ¡por supuesto!" (*La niña*, 51) [Let it hereby be recorded and summarized: I was chosen, along with four other young women, as a strategy of war. A deal between chieftains and powerful foreign lords. This fortune falls to me because I am noble and a virgin. . . . My father has destined me to become the wife of the Great Lord. . . . And I have accepted, of course!]. Aguilar's nuanced presentation of Luisa at once highlights her position as a pawn of powerful men ("caciques y los poderosos señores") and her awareness—and acceptance—of that role ("he consentido"). However, that her declaration of consent is followed by the phrase "¡por supuesto!" is significant, for it reveals that Luisa's assent is a mere formality expected by those who request it. Rebellion is unthinkable for Luisa, who identifies with her father's logic despite her fears.

As the vignette progresses, the indigenous woman gradually realizes that not even perfect obedience will bring her approval. Luisa will never be able to please either her family or the conquerors; favor depends not on her actions but rather on the interpretive lenses through which they perceive her. Throughout her story, Aguilar foregrounds the fundamental conflict between a woman's desire for community and the priorities of patriarchal agendas that deny them subjectivity. That there is no plausible resolution means that most of the episodes find narrative closure only with tragic endings. In the case of Luisa, the indigenous woman's alternative world of the imagination remains alive to the end, transforming reality to create a place of resistance and affirmation. As she dies, Luisa hears the celebratory songs of Tlaxcala, though those around her chant Christian prayers, and she leaves a troubling legacy that will haunt her mestiza daughter Leonor. The frequent mention of this daughter in the last pages of Luisa's story suggests a memory of resistance that persists in the colonized consciousness, troubling the next generation's recollection of the past.

The modern-day protagonist ultimately inherits this legacy. She writes to recover a knowledge of her antecedents, which cannot easily be captured in a single protagonist (as her Spanish friend wishes). Rather, their voices are distinct, contradictory, complicit, and resistant. In order to reconstruct their history, then, she must compose a fiction that is polyphonic, decentralized, one that weaves together the personal and political of her own life in the evocation of that past.

In telling the stories of these Central American women, both colonial and modern, Aguilar, like her protagonist, weaves together events of global importance and personal stories, showing their inseparability in the history of the isthmus. Aguilar consistently deconstructs the grandiose ambitions of men and focuses on the petty, personal motivations that influenced their decisions. In the retelling of history proffered by *La niña blanca,* the public/private distinction disappears from the lives of both men and women. Consequently, the imagination of what is missing in history does not just fill gaping silences in canonical Central American chronicles; it also questions the very legitimacy of the story the chronicles present as true.

Going Public

La niña blanca y los pájaros sin pies offers a fictionalized representation not only of the colonial past but also of the present reality of women writers. It describes what happens when women enter into dialogue with their present circumstances and the past that has shaped them. In this move to the speaking center fictionalized in this novel, the woman writer begins to account for her presence and thus "transforms the system," as suggested in the epigraph for this chapter. Aguilar's fictionalizations of history, like those of her contemporaries included in this study, emphasize women's participation in events of the past. In particular, Aguilar juxtaposes historical events with private stories to blur the lines between these domains for both men and women.

In depicting women's frustration and rebellion at being marginalized in all contexts, Aguilar points to the structural flaws of a patriarchal society that leaves little or no space for women's expression or fulfillment. Whether in her fictionalizations of conquest, colonization, the early modern state, or revolutionary society, she consistently foregrounds the conflicts and restrictions felt by women. Her protagonists resist objectification, but the assertion of their wills often means the loss of either social identity (in the case of Rosa Sarmiento) or physical security (in the case of the schoolteacher). The recurrent image is one of women emerging from the small spaces to which they had been confined, seeking fulfillment, and continuing to negotiate the competing claims upon their persons and affections. As in the protagonist-author of *La niña blanca y los pájaros sin pies,* the search for an understanding of their selves prompts an urgency to recover their past, in order that they might have lives that are both publicly and privately meaningful.

Chapter 4

"Local Histories and Global Designs"
in Tatiana Lobo's Narratives

[The subaltern woman] . . . tends to be absent from the documentary
archives, and to write her history has to involve a particular effort of re-
trieval, or . . . a particular effort of historical imagination.
                                        —Robert J. C. Young, *Colonial Desire*

THE WORKS OF Tatiana Lobo represent a "particular effort of re-
trieval and historical imagination" to discover subalterns in the colonial past of Central America.[1] While Alegría, Belli, and Aguilar all
fictionalize the past to recuperate women's history, their protagonists
tend to be literate women relegated to the margins of society because
of their gender. Lobo shares the same interest in women and the recuperation of memory. However, she introduces into her stories a cast
of indigenous, African, and mestiza women. Her historical imaginations bring to the foreground both women's problems and also those
of gendered subalterns. As Robert Young has observed, these are
figures almost completely erased in the archives of the colonizer.

As the narratives of Alegría, Belli, and Aguilar demonstrate, the incorporation of women and other marginalized groups into the story

of the past reclaims the dynamism present in the colony and the nation. Their fictions counter the monolithic colonial and national representations that made these people the first of many *desaparecidos* (disappeared)[2] in the isthmus and suppressed their history to promote various political agendas. As other texts recuperate a women's tradition in Central America, Lobo's fictional narratives restore subaltern lives to history, recreating a dialogue from the silences and lacunae of previous texts. In the process, her stories deconstruct the images, ideals, and myths that have been important in the constitution of national history and the identities founded upon that history.

In my analysis of Lobo's narratives, I consider key aspects of her fictionalizations of history—in particular, their dialogic nature and their recuperation of alternative knowledges, signs, and stories. In Lobo's texts, subaltern memories are textually reconstructed in fiction and juxtaposed with hegemonic representations of history. Her depiction of the conflicted border between knowledges makes visible Central America's marginalized inhabitants, notably subaltern women and also reveals the maneuvers of colonialism that relegated them to the peripheries.

The concern with history and with the marginalized surfaces in each of the books Lobo has published: *Tiempo de claveles* (1990), an eclectic collection of short stories; *Asalto al paraíso* (1992), her first historical novel; *Entre Dios y el diablo* (1993); *Calypso* (1996), her second novel; *Negros y blancos: Todo mezclado* (1997), a history of race co-authored with Mauricio Meléndez; and *El año del laberinto* (2000), another historical novel. As the works reconsider three centuries of Costa Rican history (eighteenth century to the present day), they problematize especially the representation of the marginalized and subalterns.

Latin Americanist Ileana Rodríguez holds that subalternity is a fluid concept, noting that there are various incarnations of subalternity among Central American writers ("Rethinking," 13). For Lobo the subaltern is the ethnic Other of Central America; she is indigenous, black, mestiza. In looking at Lobo's texts, I am interested in the manner in which the gendered subaltern appears and the possibilities Lobo presents for her representation in fiction. What are the strategies for presenting marginalized individuals and for problematizing their absence (or scarcity) in the historical record? Furthermore, how are the demands of the genre (the novel, the short story) adapted to the consideration of this "new" subject? And perhaps most important for my analysis, what processes does the subaltern's inclusion in history reveal?

In Lobo's fiction there are numerous points of intersection with the concepts of M. M. Bakhtin, Homi K. Bhabha, Walter Mignolo, and Robert J. C. Young, theorists who have addressed questions of language, desire, and colonial conflicts. For example, Bakhtin's famous essay "Discourse in the Novel" argues that the nature of language is dialogic, that centripetal and centrifugal forces create a dynamic linguistic milieu in human societies. The concept has interesting implications when employed in postcolonial analysis. It also provides a means of understanding the tension in Lobo's texts, as they represent past and present colonialities.

In colonial projects, the scribes, conquerors, and priests find a resisting Other that they must politically and rhetorically strip of agency and legitimacy. Colonial discourse expresses the centrist desires of empire (or the modern state), suppressing and denying the colonized, in order to assert and defend the universality of the imperial worldview. At the same time, however, this discourse has the unintended effect of acknowledging the power of those other languages, cultures, and knowledge systems. In recreating colonial moments, Lobo's works constantly emphasize this tension, revealing the limitations, inconsistencies, and frustrations of imperial desire.

Of further import for the interpretation of Lobo's narratives are Bakhtin's notes on linguistic hybridity. Bakhtin defines hybridization as "a mixture of two social languages within the limits of a single utterance, an encounter, within the arena of an utterance, between two different linguistic consciousnesses, separated from one another by an epoch, by social differentiation or by some other factor" (358). Later in the same essay he notes that "the novelistic hybrid is *an artistically organized system for bringing different languages in contact with one another,* a system having as its goal the illumination of one language by means of another, the carving-out of a living image of another language" (361; emphasis in original). Bakhtin's observation offers a key to understanding Lobo's texts, especially since Bakhtin understood language to be fundamentally rooted in culture. Lobo's postcolonial narratives are novelistic hybrids. Unlike other hybrids, such as colonial texts and narratives of imperial desire, her works do not carve out a "living image of another language" or culture to show its inadequacy, barbarism, or lack of sophistication. Quite to the contrary, Lobo manipulates different discourses to highlight "conflicts in the sphere of signs," to borrow Mignolo's phrase (14).

Drawing upon Bakhtin's work, both Bhabha and Young elaborated the concept of hybridization in the context of postcolonial studies. As he reads Bakhtin's notion of hybridization, Young emphasizes that the "double-voiced, hybridized discourse serves a purpose, whereby each voice can unmask the other" (21). Lobo cultivates just such a hybridized discourse in her text, making the voiceless women of history textually present in order to unmask the discourse of authority. Her historical fiction on the colonial period reflects a fundamental understanding of the irony of colonial texts, that is, that the very documents meant to subjugate and control are testament to the persistence of alternative knowledges of the world. These knowledges are held by people who have neither enjoyed colonial power nor embraced its logic. Their traces in legal proceedings and ecclesiastical records belie a very different reality than that which has been promulgated by traditional historiography. In her fictions, Lobo reconstructs the power struggles visible between the lines of official histories, exploring especially the place of women, indigenous people, and Afro-Latin Americans in Costa Rican history.

Discovering the cultural heterogeneity present in colonial and modern Central America allows Lobo to deconstruct and reinscribe the events of history. For Lobo, revealing the hybridity in language and culture is central in the construction of this new comprehension of the past. According to Young, "hybridity becomes the moment in which the discourse of colonial authority loses its univocal grip on meaning and finds itself open to the trace of the language of the other" (22). The critic is thus able "to trace complex movements of disarming alterity in the colonial text" (22). In seductive and subversive narratives, Lobo traces the *unsuccessful* disarming of alterity and reveals an altogether different version of the past.

In the Spanish American context, colonial texts (frequently the product of legal and moral qualms of the Spanish crown) generally suppress a speaking, acting Other.[3] In order to advance an imperial program of colonization and metropolitan enrichment, they objectify and commodify the conquered. Even texts that purport to present dialogue, such as the tomes of Gonzálo Fernández de Oviedo, have a dubious textual history and make the interlocutors puppets who enunciate explanations already anticipated by Europeans.[4] Texts not so obviously manipulative of the interlocutor's voice, like Fray Sahagún's folios of questions and responses contained in the *Florentine Codex,* are still tailored to a colonial agenda—in this case, its religious dimension. A struggle to suppress, discredit, or comprehend (through Western systems of thought) the dissident Other is present in all the texts. Lobo takes such sources and teases out the hidden subalterns to give them life in fiction.

In undertaking such projects, Lobo shares much in common with theorists from postcolonial and cultural studies. Together with them, she challenges Western histories of empire building and nation formation. Projects like Lobo's are not only historical or historiographic, they are also political, as Claudia Gualtieri observes: "In the rewriting of colonial adventures from a post-colonial point of view, the quest for liberation of the colonized can be effected through the transformation of history. . . . We understand ourselves through history. The challenge to official history, to its monadic, universal entities is pursued by positing what Benjamin defines as the 'hypothesis of an alternative history,' which gives voice to marginalized, silenced stories" (49). "Marginalized, silenced stories" articulate important memories. In the modern world they also contribute to what Mignolo calls an "emergent gnoseology," that is, thought that is "absorbing and displacing hegemonic forms of knowledge into the perspective of the subaltern" (12). Lobo's fiction gives the background, the behind-the-scenes view, of the "emergent gnoseology" that Mignolo discerns at present. She does this, in part, by subtly juxtaposing the hegemonic and the subaltern in her texts.

Radical Dialogues with the Colonial and National Past

The subaltern presence in Central American history has concerned Lobo for some time. She worked for several years among the indigenous peoples of Talamanca and later spent time among other marginalized individuals—Atlantic coast residents, prisoners, recovering alcoholics. Her short story collection, *Tiempo de claveles,* contains a short story, "Final del hilo," that focuses on the first female indigenous protagonist she rendered in fiction. Like much of Lobo's subsequent writing, the story highlights the difficulty, if not the impossibility, of the incorporation of the subaltern into dominant society.

Lobo's first novel, *Asalto al paraíso,* highlights many of the same difficulties of cultural contact. Punctuated by irony, *Asalto al paraíso* engages in a humorous and subversive dialogue with the texts that are its colonial informants. In a conscious mimicry of the Spanish American chronicle, each chapter begins with a heading of the sort typically given in the canonical works of colonial Latin America. The titles purportedly summarize the chapter contents, but more often than not in *Asalto,* they contain subtle jabs at the dominant culture of the era.

The entirety of the book functions in this dialogic fashion, in which the text blends "a healthy respect for the master's discourse with an unwillingness to be seduced by the *maestro*" (Castillo, 300). In the midst of Lobo's resistant reading of history, the gendered subaltern appears and acts, though she may not actually speak.

The "master's discourse" in colonial Central America provides the raw material for Lobo's third narrative project, *Entre Dios y el diablo*. Based on archival material and bearing the ambiguous subtitle *Crónicas* (Chronicles), the book spans an entire century—the first crónica is dated 1713, and the last ends in 1813—in its presentation of women through Bourbon bureaucratic trails in the archives of Costa Rica. The book is a fictional elaboration of the stories of several women, each of whom for one reason or another found herself entangled in the legal niceties of the empire. The narrative constantly highlights the difficulties suffered by women in the ecclesiastical and civil courts and confronts the reader with their complete subjection in a system always already prejudiced against their claims. Often voiceless even in the testimonies collected, the women all but disappeared from the historical record, having captivated the interest of authorities only in their transgressions of boundaries and their roles (as objects) in plays of fortune and power.

Calypso, Lobo's second novel, turns to the twentieth century and a situation of internal colonization and growing globalization. It focuses on the development of one small town on the Atlantic coast of Costa Rica. Organized around three generations of women and the omnipresent figure of Lorenzo, an "invader" from the central valley, the novel spans the approximately forty years in which the Switzerland of Central America developed. Like Gabriel García Márquez's *Cien años de soledad* (1967), the novel explores multiple generations of the same family, contains moments of magical realism, and questions the notion of history and representation.

Finally, though I do not consider them at length here, it bears mentioning that Lobo's recent publications, *Negros y blancos* and *El año del laberinto,* also have historical preoccupations. *Negros y blancos* systematically dismantles the myth of whiteness in Costa Rica, tracing the genealogies of a number of prominent families back to their enslaved African ancestors. Appearing at a politically sensitive moment in the late 1990s when elements of Costa Rican society complained about Nicaraguans arriving and "negreando el país" [turning the country black], *Negros y blancos* continues the same iconoclasm of Lobo's earlier works. It also portrays the daily struggles of slaves and the complex imbrication of slavery in the national past. In dismantling the image of the nation as an agrarian family (an idea that began circulation in the 1940s), Lobo's text joins a chorus of voices criticizing the Costa Rican government and society at the dawn of the twenty-first century.

In *El año del laberinto,* Lobo turns from one marginalized group to the next to tell the story of a nineteenth-century crime of passion, the murder of a woman in 1894. In doing so, she paints a portrait of politics, patriarchal biases, and the lives of women, both upper class and poor. Like *Asalto* and *Entre Dios y el diablo,* the book parts from a single historical event. It reaches in concentric circles beyond it to find a world of political intrigue and corruption. Taking on the sacred national identity once again, Lobo mounts a different story from a series of past events, plotting them to reveal how history may be constructed according to distinct priorities.

"Final del hilo": Prototype of Later Narratives

Considering an early story by Lobo proves helpful in understanding her most salient techniques: "alternative emplotment" and the juxtaposition of discourses. She makes the construction of both transparent in "Final del hilo." The short story from *Tiempo de claveles* concerns an indigenous woman and her Spanish-speaking, mestizo *compañero.* A prototype of later narratives, it introduces in six pages many of the preoccupations and narrative strategies Lobo employs in her novels.

"Final del hilo" begins in the voice of the mestizo Roderico, who has set out through the mountains during the dry season. He makes clear his departure from civilization, noting that he has left behind "la yunta y el ganado, la cobija y mis hermanos" [yoke and cattle, shelter and siblings] to wander in "las montañas salvajes" (53) [the wild mountains]. Beside a river, he encounters Aminta, a young indigenous woman he later takes as his wife.

Significantly, as the text opens, Aminta's grandmother dies, cutting the young woman off from the memories of her culture. Lobo makes clear the implications of her death in Aminta's plea: "Abuela, no te mueras. . . . Abuela, ésta tu nieta no tendrá nadie que le ayude a tejer la vida" (53) [Grandmother, don't die. . . . Grandmother, this granddaughter of yours won't have anyone to help her weave her life]. Shortly after, Roderico enters her world and introduces Aminta to a tradition to which she does not belong. As the plot progresses, the tension between cultures intensifies for Aminta, upon whose person Roderico acts out his desires.

Throughout the text, Lobo juxtaposes two discourses, Aminta's interior discourse and that of Roderico. This is a technique Lobo adapts in later texts, such as *Entre Dios y el diablo* and *Calypso,* where focalized passages often play off one another to show the contest over interpretive power. In "Final del hilo," the interweaving of narrative voices first highlights the blurring of differences as Roderico and Aminta come together as lovers. Lobo uses sentences with the same syntactical configuration to communicate this union, and the two narrative voices join in (apparent) harmony to elaborate lyrical passages. For example, in Roderico's voice, there is this passage: "Tanto tiempo ha pasado que no hay nada fuera de su cuerpo, donde yo me sumerjo junto con el río, los pájaros y la lluvia" (54) [So much time has passed that there is nothing besides her body, where I merge myself with the river, the birds, and the rain]. It is immediately followed by

Aminta's thoughts: "Tanto tiempo pasó que éramos el árbol, la lluvia y el fuego. . . . Tanto tiempo pasó que su carne se hizo oscura como la mía y yo me fui poniendo blanca como las flores de la quebrada" (54–55) [So much time passed that we were tree, rain, fire. . . . so much time passed that his flesh turned dark like mine and I began turning white like the flowers of the stream]. The juxtaposition of narratives hints at possible utopias, but the change in verb tenses in Aminta's indicate that any hope of blissful union has already been lost.

The technique of counterpoint later highlights the growing conflict between Roderico and Aminta. Although the couple meets and initially lives in the mountains, when Aminta becomes pregnant, Roderico moves her to town. He explains, "somos gente para vivir entre la gente" (56) [we are people meant to live among people], and with that he packs up Aminta, buys her a new dress, and takes her to town. Once there he forbids her to leave the house because he does not like the way men look at her (57). Pregnant, lonely, and in unfamiliar territory, Aminta invents a dialogue with her grandmother as she gradually loses all physical connections to her culture. Her discourse reveals her desire to leave in order to survive as a person; Roderico's, his insistence that she stay to warm his food and bed. All the signs of her culture removed, Aminta is left a prisoner stripped of her identity. A nonbeing with no alternative but death, Aminta kills her husband, "para que [Roderico] no se diera cuenta que Aminta ya no estaba allá [so that [Roderico] would not notice that Aminta was no longer there]," and then throws herself into the river (59).

The narrative foregrounds not only the clash of cultures, but also the struggle over the subjectivity of the gendered subaltern. Aminta suffers psychologically because she is an Indian stripped of her culture and because as a woman she is subjected completely to the will of her partner. In a very short story about three generations, Lobo dramatizes the changes that occurred over time in Costa Rica. In particular, she emphasizes the implicit violence with which agrarian life (ruled by patriarchal concerns) replaced the alternative order Aminta and her grandmother represented at the beginning of the story.

The preoccupation with subalterns and women evidenced in "Final del hilo" appears in Lobo's other texts. In them, Lobo elaborates more fully the interaction of cultures, the regulation of women, and the prejudices of the historical record in dealing with the presence of the Others of Central America. In order to accomplish this revision of history, Lobo utilizes textual strategies similar to those employed in "Final del hilo," developing a style of counterpoint that brings out inconsistencies and tensions in human relationships, as well as the historiographic record.

Women and Men in the Contact Zone: Asalto al paraíso

Like "Final del hilo," *Asalto al paraíso* is a fictional re-presentation of colonial Costa Rica. It is carefully constructed to reveal the ambiguities of the epoch glossed over in history books but played out with profundity in the lives of individuals in the region. As such, it is part of an attempt to decolonize knowledge and memory, fictionalizing a past long suspected and only recently given textual elaboration. Though all of Lobo's fictions share the same interest in the decolonization of memory, *Asalto* in particular focuses on themes identified by cultural studies scholars like Mignolo and Mary Louise Pratt. It imagines "contestatory expressions from the site of imperial intervention [and] the critique of empire encoded ongoingly on the spot," insisting on "the story of another letter" (Pratt, 2). Especially in this novel, Lobo writes to recover the memory of contact zones, those "social spaces where disparate cultures meet, clash, and grapple with each other, often in highly asymmetrical relations of domination and subordination" (Pratt, 4). In *Asalto* the contact zone is colonial Costa Rica, particularly Cartago and Talamanca, during the 1700s. In Costa Rica, as in all of Spanish America, the eighteenth century was a time in which Spanish expansion pushed further into the interior of the Americas and thus precipitated another round of cultural clashes.

In order to communicate the dynamics of the contact zone, *Asalto al paraíso* relates two parallel stories. One is concerned with the indigenous mobilization for rebellion in Talamanca and the other (more or less simultaneous) one revolves around the life of the protagonist. The novel is structured in chapters that carry parodic headings in calligraphy reminiscent of those found in colonial texts. For example, the second chapter begins with the imposing heading, "De los primeros días que pasa Pedro Albarán en un lugar de las Indias Occidentales, cuyos habitantes se le antojan chismosos, lenguarraces y viperinos" (13) [On the first days Pedro Albarán spends in a place in the West Indies, whose inhabitants he feels to be gossipy, foul-mouthed, and viperish]. In alternating chapters, the novel juxtaposes the two narrative representations of the same place, time, and events. Very brief chapters present the indigenous preparations for war, while the majority of the text centers about the life of protagonist Pedro Albarán, a fugitive from the Inquisition who arrives in the New World and finds work as a scribe in the *cabildo* (seat of municipal government) of Cartago.

Inasmuch as it is the story of Pedro, *Asalto al paraíso* is a novel about transculturation, "the mutual transformation of cultures, in particular of the European by the native" (Rowe and Schelling, 18). The date of the novel's publication (1992) corresponds to a moment of heightened awareness of processes of cultural transformation in Latin America.[5] Just like the debates over Columbus's voyage, Lobo's endeavors in fiction question the nature of social configurations and of the discourses that construct them. *Asalto*, in particular, undermines the vision of colonial reality and proposes a new understanding of not only past but also present human relationships. Lobo accomplishes this by overtly challenging the historical record and by subtly configuring a fictional world that supplements the "real" one posited by authoritative texts.

In *Asalto,* Lobo shows particular concern to represent the diversity within marginalized groups. Her text incorporates priests, governors, and captains, as well as the sundry individuals at their margins: unsatisfied wives and mistresses, slaves, prostitutes, fugitives of the Inquisition, disillusioned neophytes, and numerous indigenous people. Her recognition of heteroglossia, not just in the colony but also within the ranks of the colonized, defies an authoritarian discourse that would deny the centrifugal forces always at work in society and emphasizes in its stead the clashes and transformations engendered by colonial projects.

Asalto al paraíso is also concerned with a particularly problematic time in the Spanish empire, during which the wars of succession in Europe weakened the Spanish imperial hold on her colonies. In the midst of metropolitan confusion and chaos, the indigenous peoples of Talamanca organized their uprising, and the colonizers, their reprisal. This is the historical moment fictionalized by the text.

However, is the colonial violence against Indians of Talamanca the "assault on paradise" to which the text refers? Should one interpret the title and text in the style of the Black Legend, viewing the Indians as good and innocent natives oppressed by evil Spanish colonizers? The referent of the title is superficially problematic because there is very little that resembles paradise in colonial Costa Rica, much less in this representation of it.[6] Furthermore, such a facile interpretation does not seem consistent with the complex world of the text, which is dedicated more to the deconstruction of binaries than to inversions of them. The title is perhaps better understood as a parody of the notion of a European assault on an indigenous paradise. The conception of historical events as an assault on paradise presumes a certain unified and static Spanish identity, one that Lobo discounts at length, and a similarly integrated and idyllic indigenous reality. Furthermore, to postulate the European arrival as an attack on paradise is to cast the struggle in much starker shades than the reality of the Conquest warrants. Neither was the Spanish response to Talamanca an assault—it was illegal, unorganized, and woefully disappointing—nor was the indigenous world of Central America a paradise. The title can also be read as a self-referential commentary on the book in Costa Rican cultural life, that is, *Asalto al paraíso* is just what it declares itself to be—an attack on the Costa Rican image of a democratic utopian community. The revelation of the colonial violence responsible for securing that appearance of paradise is a strike against the foundations of both a cherished national myth and identity.

Without doubt, the novel consistently plots an assault on accepted representations of history, deconstructing the neat worlds humans have fashioned to make sense of their existences. This is seen at the story level in the relation of Pedro's utopian community on the beach, which he maintains by being willfully blind to the troubled political and social situation of the colony. Finally, his imagined paradise collapses in the contest for territory and power realized by the Indians and the colonizers. Unable to maintain the ebbing illusion of tranquility, Pedro is forced from his solitude into an active confrontation of the conflicts within himself.

The entire text is then an attack—not just on our perceptions of history but also on the very notion of paradise, of the human capacity to maintain a viable and coherent center sufficient to quiet conflicts of identity and allegiances. The story of Pedro suggests the existence of a human society in which individuals and actions are determined and perceived in a dynamic that requires constant negotiation. As it tells the story of a contradictory hero in a dystopic world, *Asalto al paraíso* not only questions authoritative discourse but also affirms the possibility of meaningful contact between human beings. Contact between cultures provokes social clashes, as well as internal conflicts for the individuals concerned, but it is also able to facilitate real and sometimes positive change in human communities.

In illuminating the history of the contact zone, *Asalto* relies on an interesting narrative technique and novelistic structure. Like "Final del hilo," the novel juxtaposes narratives to foreground contradictions and to force the reader to construct and revise her own understanding of the colony. As mentioned earlier, the novel alternates chapters on colonial Cartago and on Pedro with brief chapters that give an inside view of the indigenous preparations for war under the direction of Pa-brú Presbere. Within the "colonial" narrative, there are two distinct narrators: one, el Risueño, intra- and homodiegetic (located within the story), and the other extra- and heterodiegetic (outside the story). The multiplication of narrative voices constructs interpretations only to deconstruct them later. The reader must therefore take an active role and constantly confront issues of representation at the level of both the story and the storytelling.

The narrator in the first person, el Risueño, provides a counterpoint to the third person narrative, frequently focalized in Pedro, and proffers to the reader an interpretation of Pedro within the story itself. However, the voice of the extradiegetic narrator is a far cry from the omniscient narrator of tradition, for it acknowledges uncertainty in its own discourse throughout the novel. For instance, after elaborating a series of facts that only an omniscient narrator could "know," this narrator comments at the beginning of the novel, "si la Lorenzana vio a Pedro en el atrio de la iglesia parroquial es poco probable" (1) [it is highly unlikely that Lorenzana saw Pedro in the vestibule of the parish church]. Statements such as this suggest that even narration is contingent and that absolute certainty is never possible, even when discussing quotidian historical events.

In addition to the decentralized and multivoiced narrative, the novel also employs a nonlinear structure that frequently recurs to prolepses and analepses (flash-forwards and flashbacks). Such a structure demands an active collaboration on the part of the reader, who is never permitted a stable image of the events or the protagonist and must weave together strings of narrative to form a coherent understanding of the plot. In Lobo's new historical novel there is no authoritative voice to reconcile discrepancies and resolve ambiguities; rather there is an insistence on the negotiation of meaning at the level of both story and discourse.

The lack of an authoritative interpretation is never more glaringly obvious than in the presentation of the subaltern woman in the novel. She is the silent figure around whom the plot revolves. Like her real-life historical referent in colonial Latin America, the indigenous woman is a key figure in the process of transculturation, and *Asalto* is her story as much as it is that of Pedro. However, the subaltern woman in *Asalto* has no voice and thus no testimonial authority of her own; she is quite literally la Muda (the Mute). Her identity is always mediated by Pedro or some other Spanish male figure, usually by means of focalized passages or reported speech in the text. Always appearing through the filter of others, she has no possibility of self-representation in language.

The difficulty of Pedro in describing his experiences with la Muda, either to himself or in dialogue with others, emphasizes again the gap between the subaltern and even a marginalized member of the dominant culture. Though Pedro is not an insider in colonial Costa Rica—he is, after all, a fugitive of the Inquisition—he is literate and trained in a Western textual tradition, skills that enable him to survive. He does not identify with the Spanish and mestizo culture of Cartago, but neither does he belong to the indigenous culture, nor does he speak their language. Lobo emphasizes the gap in his knowledge in the reported speech of the novel, in which Pedro frequently recurs to metaphors to speak of la Muda.[7] For Pedro, metaphorical explanations are the only adequate means to approximate la Muda, whose alterity baffles his ability to name, describe, and possess.

By directing the attention of the reader toward the frustrations of Pedro, Lobo signals the difficulty of adequately representing the subaltern woman in an alien language. For Pedro, it is simply impossible to discuss la Muda in anything other than figurative language, and he mentions frequently her "ojos de pozos profundos" [eyes like deep wells] as he discursively confronts her alterity. Consider the following passage in which Pedro describes la Muda to a friend: "A veces me parecía que la mejor figura, el mejor ejemplo para explicarla, si es que ella puede tener explicación, era la profundidad callada del océano, ese espacio desconocido al que los navegantes temen porque no la han visto nunca. . . . Ella era . . . era . . . el caos, lo pienso ahora" (173) [Sometimes it seemed that the best figure, the best example to explain her, that is, if she has any explanation at all, was the quiet profundity of the ocean, that unknown space that sailors fear because they have never seen it. . . . She was . . . she was . . . the chaos, now that I think of it]. La Muda is perceived as "chaos" by Pedro, so completely different that she pertains to another indecipherable order. Pedro is an outsider, and the muteness of la Muda frustrates any linguistic attempts to negotiate the two worlds to which they belong.

Though the novel emphasizes la Muda's permanence in a world beyond the reach of language, it does not imply that she consequently has no impact on history. Again, the sempiternal question of postcolonial studies surfaces: Can the subaltern speak? Most definitely not, at least not in this case. More important, though, Lobo asserts that she can act, and her being and doing transform the social order. Though colonial civil and ecclesiastical society make every military, political, and rhetorical effort to deny both her presence and her power, they are ultimately unsuccessful. Like Pedro's efforts at rendering la Muda in language, hegemonic discourses multiply in their attempts to create a linguistically surmountable Other, be it indigenous or African. *Asalto* carefully constructs a fictionalized representation of the limitations and power of authorities and of subalterns. And, as it signals the importance of the subaltern woman in colonial society, the novel ultimately undermines the voice of authority.

Symbol of the indigenous woman in colonial Latin America, la Muda is anonymous and silent. Her existence, however, determines the fate of many. Through her productive and reproductive powers, she prompts cultural critique and change in those who surround her. For instance, as a result of his fascination with her alterity, Juan de las Alas attempts to abandon his vocation. Citing her influence, he later dedicates himself to the evangelization and protection of the indigenous peoples of Talamanca, until he finally becomes insane. Similarly, because of his relationship with la Muda, Pedro is transformed from state functionary to fugitive once again. He abandons his government post and later frees the captured Indians from their prison in Cartago. Besides transforming associates of the church and the state, la Muda inaugurates a new order in another way; she is the mother of mestizo children. She disappears after death, but her children and the indelible mark she makes on Pedro are powerful testaments to her existence.

In her construction of la Muda, Lobo renders the indigenous woman as she appears in colonial documents and yet suggests much more than colonial texts. Lobo's representation of la Muda is a delicately managed one, faithful to both indigenous women's real historical presence and their conspicuous discursive absence in colonial texts. For instance, la Muda never speaks, and like Pedro, the reader never knows anything about her with assurance. In creating this uncertainty, Lobo not only honors the alterity of the colonial subaltern woman, she also positions the reader in the exact same space to which Pedro and the contemporary historian are relegated. Pedro knows that la Muda is central to an understanding of himself, just as the reader is given clues throughout the text that indicate the centrality of la Muda to the plot. The subaltern woman is there— there is ample testament to that fact—but she leaves no textual traces of her own.

By implication, the text suggests that the colonial Other is critical for a meaningful comprehension of the past, and yet one is confronted by the infuriating absence of her voice in the colonial record. In *Asalto* she is shown as the historical agent that she is—companion to Spanish bureaucrats (Pedro is an official scribe), mother of mestizo children, and determinant of the course of history. She is present, and contact with her effects very real change in members of the dominant culture, but she has entered discourse only in the voices of others.

Through la Muda's sister, Gerónima, the novel emphasizes the existence of an active indigenous cultural and political life in the colony. Gerónima moves between the two worlds in which she participates with greater ease than does her sister. Though Gerónima first works as a cook in the convent and later oversees the daily management of Pedro's beach camp, she continues to take part in events in the indigenous world. Unperceived by Pedro, the missionaries, and the colonial authority, hers is the habit of many of the subjugated Indians of the region. No one notices the persistence of indigenous culture and politics until there is a crisis: when the Indians step in to sell their tortillas in Cartago during the wheat shortage, when Gerónima "abruptly" announces her departure, or when rebellious groups burn the missions in Talamanca. Only then do they realize that indigenous people have all along been cultivating their crops, planning strategies of resistance, maintaining religious practices, plotting their own lives.

The text brings the existence of the two parallel worlds into focus, and the juxtaposition demythologizes the totalizing pretensions of colonial power and discourse. As the novel nears its conclusion, the two narratives converge on a single event: the uprising in Talamanca. It becomes clear that the indigenous leaders have integrated the news of European turmoil within their own interpretation of reality in order to organize and foment the uprising: "Dos reyes pelean al otro lado del mar, en la nación que llaman España, a la que tanto temes. Esos dos reyes necesitan sus armas para hacer la guerra entre ellos y para defenderse de sus enemigos, los ingleses. Los ingleses son los que vienen a robar gente y cacao, los que vienen en piraguas por el mar" (186) [Two kings fight on the other side of the sea, in the nation they call Spain, that nation you fear so much. Those two kings need weapons to make war between themselves and to defend themselves from their enemies, the English. The English are the ones who come to steal people and cacao, those that come in canoes from the sea].

Informed of the instability in Europe (Europe's "local history") and having received directions from the divining stones, el Guerrero (lit., Warrior) and Presbere prepare the Talamancan indigenous groups to drive the Spanish from the territory.

Though the novel concludes with the defeat of the uprising Presbere organized, the event does not appear as a resounding victory for the Spanish. First of all, *Asalto al paraíso* makes clear that there is no unified, univocal "Spanish" culture or civilization. Both the colonial and peninsular world are fraught with fissures on political, social, and religious levels. The military and political leaders of Cartago have neither imperial approval nor popular support for their endeavor; they are motivated by petty, local rivalries and personal greed. Having convinced men to enlist in the expedition with the (illegal) promise of indigenous slaves as a reward, local colonial officials attempt to expedite the judgment of Presbere and begin slave distribution before orders to the contrary arrive from Guatemala.

The arrival of a flock of *guacamayas* (macaws) for the duration of Presbere's trial and imprisonment in Cartago points out the possibility of multiple and vastly different interpretations of reality. Shortly after the indigenous leader is imprisoned, the guacamayas situate themselves on the rooftop of the cabildo and upset the proceedings below with raucous noises. Their "plumas multicolores, increíbles, furiosamente azules, insolentemente verdes, agresivamente rojas" [incredible, multicolored feathers—furiously blue, insolently green, aggressively red"] fascinates and terrifies the onlookers, some of whom are attacked when they attempt to capture the birds to take them home (291). This is an interesting metaphor for the indigenous resistance, especially since Presbere is associated with the guacamaya in the novel. Pedro's mestiza daughter Catarina, speaking in poetic parallelism, relates that "Pa-brú quiere decir rey de las lapas, dueño de las guacamayas" (270) [Pa-brú means king of the limpets, ruler of the macaws] and Juan de las Alas insists that they carry away the soul of Presbere after his death (314). When Pá-bru Presbere is executed, the guacamayas depart at the urging shouts of Juan; they head toward the setting sun, in accordance with indigenous expectations about the afterlife of warriors.[8]

According to Lobo's representation, what the people of Cartago perceive as simply an odd occurrence is actually an indication of the presence of an alternative reality of which they are unaware because they cannot read its signs. At the conclusion of the novel it is Catarina, the daughter of Pedro and la Muda, who appears to have the capacity to decipher and negotiate the two worlds. Catarina is the child of Pedro and la Muda, and in her person persists the indigenous culture of her mother and aunt, though she remains in the care of her father. Presbere sees either Catarina or her mother in his trance, related in the first chapter of the novel: "vio también a una niña pequeña, con ojos como pozos, que hacía callar a las piedras: criatura extraña flotando a la deriva de la vida" (12) [he also saw a small girl, with eyes like wells, who made the stones silent; a strange creature floating with the drift of life]. The refusal of the stones to speak is linked to the defeat of the Indian uprising: "Ahora las piedras estaban mudas" (234) [Now the stones were mute]. In imagining the logic of the indigenous peoples of Talamanca, *Asalto al paraíso* posits an alternative interpretation of the defeat. Furthermore, like other portions of the text, it inverts the usual order in which indigenous existence and belief are discursively adjusted to fit into a Western notion of history.

Such an imagination of the Talamanca resistance suggests a different history, one that accounts for the mutual influences of dominant and subaltern cultures. Rather than reproducing binaries, the novel suggests that transculturation and meaningful social change are possible. The transformation of Pedro from passive observer to active intercessor in the affairs of the colony particularly emphasizes this inference. The last pages of the novel focus again on the protagonist as he vividly relives in a dream his life with la Muda and the childhood of Catarina. He awakens with resolve to free the imprisoned Indians. Convinced that among those who take refuge in the shadows is the green-eyed child who is the son he abandoned, he acts, then flees Cartago with Catarina in his arms. It is the memory of la Muda and her mestizo children that catalyze the growing uneasiness of Pedro into definite action against colonial oppression. As a result of his contact with the Other, which effects his transformation, Pedro makes a definitive break from the colonial center of Cartago and himself becomes part of imperial Spain's elusive, resistant Other.

The conclusion, however, has none of the easy resolution of historical accounts. In the indigenous-centered narrative, the events are only partially visible to Presbere at the beginning, when he imagines the indigenous resistance and cannot quite foretell its conclusion. At the conclusion, ambiguities persist as el Risueño recounts the local speculations about the disappearance of Pedro. The combination of the two narratives and the conclusion in the voice of the marginalized *zapatero* [lit., cobbler] cast the final pages—the letter from the king—in a different light. The belated missive is not a document of colonial glory but rather a hollow statement of tardy approval. The authoritative discourse of the king has already been deprived of its authority by events in the colonies. In the words of Bakhtin, "it becomes simply an object, a *relic*, a *thing*" (344; emphasis in original). Reality was not what the king imagined. Indeed, *Asalto* suggests that in the contact zone, representations of reality are never certain, always contested.

One Hundred Years of History:
Entre Dios y el diablo *in the Colony*

Just as *Asalto al paraíso* used subaltern lives to highlight the ignorance of traditional history, *Entre Dios y el diablo* brings women's lives to center stage to reveal the contradictions of history. The first edition of *Entre Dios* features a telling cover illustration in which faceless women carry a statue of the Virgin on their shoulders. Other faceless women watch from a balcony above. Despite their different positions and postures, they all resemble one another and the Virgin they elevate in the procession. Without faces, they are indistinguishable, identifiable only as female participants and onlookers in a religious observance.

The colonial record that informs the text of *Entre Dios y el diablo* contains many such figures of women, the details of whose lives are never fully sketched out in records always concerned with other more "important" matters. *Entre Dios* engages this legacy of absence. It takes the barely distinguishable traces of women in colonial records and imagines the details these lack. The series of crónicas that comprise the text are fictionalized accounts of lives women might have led in colonial Costa Rica.

Drawing on one hundred years of colonial archival records in *Entre Dios,* Lobo works to restore the faces of ordinary women to the history of the nation. She explicitly cites information contained in records and signals to the reader the poetic liberties taken to produce a coherent narrative, thereby emphasizing the limitations of traditional history. Her narrative strategy is particularly interesting because it makes obvious the confines of the colonial record and also reiterates the difficulty confronted by women in history.

By focusing on colonial women, Lobo has chosen protagonists who do not have complete stories. In writing their lives, she alerts the reader to the gaps she at times fills in with suppositions. The following example from "Josefa Teresa Martínez, o La adúltera, 1731," illustrates this technique well:

> El porqué Teresa, casada con un hombre que en edad podía ser su padre, se arriesgó por el tortuoso sendero del adulterio con otro que podía ser su abuelo, queda entre los imponderables humanos. No es ella quien nos cuenta la historia siguiente, así que sus verdaderos motivos seguirán siendo un misterio, y solo nos queda la especulación con base en los datos de las genealogías de Cartago y de la narración que hace su marido, Vicente Andrés Polo. (55) [The reason why Teresa, who was married to a man old enough to be her father, risked

herself in the torturous path of adultery with another man, this one old enough to be her grandfather, remains among the imponderables of humanity. It is not she who tells the following story, so her true motives will continue to be a mystery, and all that is left to us is speculation based on data from the genealogies of Cartago and on the account given by her husband, Vicente Andrés Polo.]

The enticing introduction communicates succinctly in the first two lines the intrigue awaiting explanation—a love triangle involving a woman and two older men. It then immediately informs the reader that the mystery of why will never be solved. The story is not that of the woman, and she does not tell it; therefore, her motives will never be known.

Story after story reiterates the same fact: that the colonial records only hint at the stories of women; they never offer a complete vision of women's lives and motivations. In archival and genealogical data, there is no coherent history of women in the colony. Rather, the history is necessarily fragmented because colonial scribes, clerks, and chroniclers always portrayed women as supporting actors in the male-centered drama of history, never as subjects in their own right.

As Gerda Lerner has pointed out, "history as traditionally recorded and interpreted by historians has been, in fact, the history of the activities of men ordered by male values" (*Majority*, 168). Women, therefore, "appear only as marginal 'contributors' to human development" (169). And so it goes in the colonial archives of Costa Rica. For instance, in the story of "Juana Delgado, o El incesto, 1725," the victim of sexual abuse is not seen as a victim but rather as the "cabo suelto, pieza faltante en el ajedrez, vacío en el rompecabezas, incómoda mancha que ensucia la limpieza inmaculada del procedimiento" (51) [the loose end, the missing piece in a game of chess, the blank space in the puzzle, the disquieting stain that dirties the immaculate purity of the proceedings]. In an imperial and ecclesiastical legal code always already prejudiced against them, women do not exist as human subjects. They thus rarely appear as such in the meticulously catalogued notes of colonial scribes.

Accordingly, the women of *Entre Dios y el diablo* receive discursive attention only because they had the bad fortune to draw attention to themselves and merit inquiry by ecclesiastical or state courts. Traditional history found it sufficient to record their names, resolve legal questions, and return the women to their proper state of anonymity. Faithful to their sources, the vignettes of *Entre Dios y el diablo* comply with this pattern—to a degree. Each episode begins with the first appearance of the woman in written documents and concludes with the last traces of her existence in the archival records, usually an entry on the birth or death of children or a fine paid to resolve the dispute in question. However, the pages in between communicate what is and is not known in such a way as to demystify the truth claims of the documents that inform the project.

Not only because of the stories it tells but because of the technique it employs, the work as a whole is significant in its contribution to women's history. As the author writes, "La historia de la mujer costarricense está por escribirse" (11) [The history of the Costa Rican woman is yet to be written]. However, the writing of such a history presents several problems. Lobo makes certain that her reader becomes aware of them. Though archival records are rich sources of information, they tend to omit "the actual experience of women in the past" (Lerner, *Majority*, 153). Thus, women appear as small blips on screens that show the important events of society; only insofar as they relate to business transactions, property disputes, and the maintenance of religious orthodoxy do women appear at all in most records.

Their brief appearances, suggests *Entre Dios y el diablo*, are enough to affirm that the women who populated the colony looked nothing like the stereotype propagated by history: "Cualquiera que haya sido el lugar que [las mujeres] ocuparon en el sistema de división social, ninguna se parece al estereotipo que el mito nos legó"

(11) [Whatever might have been the place that women occupied in the system of social organization, not a single woman resembled the stereotype that myth bequeathed to us]. How, then, does *Entre Dios y el diablo* expose stereotypes and explode the myths of the past? What is the alternative vision it produces to supplement the historical record that it demonstrates as lacking?

Central American reality was very different from the stereotype promulgated by church and state; as Lobo asserts,

> aquella señora vestida de riguroso negro, los ojos siempre bajos, siempre atada al fogón de su cocina, beata de mil candelas al santo de su devoción, esposa frígida que hacía el amor al mismo tiempo que desgranaba las cuentas del rosario, solo existió en el ideal que la Iglesia trató de imponer con muy pobres resultados, como lo prueba la larga lista de hijos ilegítimos que engorda los libros de bautizos de esos años. (11) [that woman dressed in severe black, eyes always downcast, always tied to the hearth of the kitchen, piously dedicated with a thousand candles to the cult of her chosen saint, the frigid wife who made love while she said the rosary, only existed in the ideal the Church tried to impose, with very poor results, as is proved by the long list of illegitimate children that fatten the baptismal books of those years.]

Lobo makes logical questions obvious in the text. For instance, if the stereotype of the frigid, devout, and submissive woman were true, why are there so many baptismal records for illegitimate children? Their existence—like the existence of a mestizo population—reveals much more about the dynamics of the colony than the historical record openly admits.

Furthermore, if the historical record is revealed to be lacking with regard to information about at least half of the population, it is a partial history and not the comprehensive, authoritative one it is often claimed. Again, as Lerner suggests, women's history demands a paradigm shift; historical studies must ask different questions if they are to avoid this traditional gender bias (*Majority*, 180). The interrogation of notions of history posited by *Entre Dios y el diablo* in turn problematizes the national identity founded upon such partial histories. If neither the past nor the nation is what it claims to be, then perhaps there is room now for the negotiation of identities and desires, especially by groups relegated to categories and stereotypes.

Calypso: *Counterpoints and Responses to Modernity*

The stereotyped Other appears again in *Calypso,* a novel that explores the social, cultural, and economic dynamics of a fictional town on the Atlantic coast of Costa Rica. This effort of historical imagination considers another contact zone of the more recent past: the underdeveloped coast at the margin of the modern state. Like the calypsos to which the title refers, the text engages the discourse of the masters—political and literary—to offer an alternative rendition of events and to affirm the resilience of human communities.

In historical and political terms, the culturally and linguistically distinct Atlantic coast is an area that has long remained at the margins of Costa Rican national discourse. The Atlantic coast was barely considered by Central Valley elites, that is, until it was coveted by foreign entrepreneurs, first in tropical fruit ventures and then in tourism, drug trafficking, and petroleum exploration.[9] The region appears sporadically in the literature of the twentieth century, and then often in the service of a nationalistic ideology. And since it is populated by English-speaking peoples of African descent who have a different history than the rest of the nation, the region itself has never shared much of the symbolic currency of the modern republic of Costa Rica.

In the rhetoric of politicians and writers from the Central Valley, the Atlantic coast often appears as an underdeveloped region populated by blacks who are easy prey for American capitalists. One of the most famous Costa Rican novels, *Mamita Yunai* (1941) by Carlos Luis Fallas, gives a vision of a backward territory of exploited people in need of socialist organization to deliver them from corrupt elites and foreign entrepreneurs. As the book begins, the narrator describes his move to "la provincia de Limón, en el litoral Atlántico de mi país, feudo de la United Fruit Company, el poderoso trust norteamericano" (11) [Limón Province, on the Atlantic coast of my country, a feudal territory of the United Fruit Company, the powerful North American trust]. Though sympathetic to the marginalized and exploited workers it defends, Fallas's anti-imperialist discourse creates a Manichean representation that stresses economic marginalization and class difference rather than the cultural dynamics of the region.

Similarly, in Joaquín Gutiérrez's classic *Murámonos, Federico* (1973), Limón is an alien territory of heat, disease, and racial segregation. Consider Federico's sarcastic response to his anxious wife just before their move to the coast:

> Y también hay leprosos. Y con el calor se derriten los sesos y se te salen por las orejas y al negro del carretón de la basura se le está poniendo la cara rosada a parchones de una enfermedad muy rara y los gringos tienen su club aparte y su balneario aparte y te invitan a lo más una vez al año por caridad a sus fiestas. (Gutiérrez, 54) [And there are also lepers. And with the heat your brains melt and come out your ears and the face of the black man with the garbage wagon is turning pink in patches from a very strange illness and the gringos have their separate club and their separate spa and they invite you, out of charity, at most once a year to their parties.]

This novel from the 1970s at once mocks and perpetuates the image of an impenetrable territory foreign to the inhabitants of the more civilized Central Valley. The mention of social division emphasizes the inequality and exploitation suffered by the faceless *negros* of the region.

Lobo's representation is a very different one, not ordered by Marxist thought or anti-imperialist, nationalist concerns. Rather, her text emphasizes the persistence and adaptation of the human community as it participates in the larger political and economic structures of the second half of the twentieth century. Her imagination of the community of Parima Bay offers a unique perspective on cultural and social change as the result of internal colonization, modernity, and globalization. Taking as its subject the "foundation" of the community around the general store opened by Lorenzo Parima, an outsider from the Central Valley, the novel turns the standard narratives of colonization, foundation, and progress inside out. This is accomplished by interweaving the story of Lorenzo Parima and the women of the extended Scarlet family in an innovative and decentralized narrative. Such a structure enables Lobo to highlight the cultural adaptation and resistance of the community and of the women who form its backbone.

In *Calypso,* Lobo dismantles the binaries and dichotomies that have served as the building blocks of national myths and identities. Her text emphasizes what Mignolo calls "colonial semiosis," or "conflicts in the sphere of signs" that occur with coloniality (14). For the Atlantic coast town in the novel, Lorenzo is the harbinger of Western progress, gradually introducing electricity, telecommunications, and other modern infrastructure. However, Lobo posits that these changes are motivated by the desires and insecurities of the modernizer; they do not result from economic or scientific imperatives. Rather, Lorenzo develops a logic a posteriori to justify the changes. Thus, the text points out the contingency of totalizing colonialist discourses, and it offers an alternative emplotment of Costa Rican development in the twentieth century.

Through the incorporation of multiple discourses, the novel juxtaposes Lorenzo's rationalizations with perspectives that discredit them. Lorenzo Parima is a newcomer to the Atlantic coast from the Central Valley, a place he left because of his distaste for agricultural labor and the paucity of land available for distribution among the siblings of his family. Once on the coast, he quickly allies himself with the popular black stevedore Plantintáh Robinson, with whom he enters into a business venture financed by the inheritance of

Plantintáh's girlfriend Amanda Scarlet. He proceeds to eliminate his partner from the business, pursue Amanda, kill Plantintáh, and expand his monopoly on commerce and transportation. Lorenzo's obsessive desire for the Scarlet women reproduces itself in each generation. The novel threads the character's stories together to show Lorenzo's strategies for control and the various ways the community co-opts and subverts his plans.

Though the focus of the novel is the community of Parima Bay, the narrative emphasizes both local history and global designs, imbedding the events of the story into a larger narrative of increasing globalization. Lobo rejects an essentializing narrative that would represent Parima Bay as a static and culturally pure community. Instead, she constructs a small world whose borders are fluid and uncertain. Her techniques are strikingly similar to those favored by theorists of ethnography. For instance, anthropologist George Marcus comments on the challenge of producing a text "once the line between the local worlds of subjects and the global world of systems becomes radically blurred" (171). He notes that it is possible to use "sequential narrative and the effect of simultaneity" or to construct "the text around a strategically selected locale, treating the system as background" (172). Lobo uses both tactics to show the permeability of borders and the repercussions of world events in economically and politically marginalized areas.

The novel begins by linking two events that occur at the same time and share a common theme: "una invasión de territorios ajenos" (11) [an invasion of foreign lands]. According to the text, "ni Hitler ni Parima conocían la existencia de uno y otro y cada quien iniciaba una invasión a territorios ajenos, a su manera y según sus posibilidades" (11) [neither Hitler nor Parima knew of the existence of the other, and each one began an invasion of foreign lands, each in his own way and according to his possibilities]. The linking of events in Central America and Europe accomplishes at least two tasks: it gives a temporal frame of reference for the story and immediately guides the reader's interpretation of Lorenzo by comparing him to Hitler. Throughout the text similar allusions to international events are made, showing the increasing connection of Parima Bay to world economic and political systems.

Though the first few pages of narrative revolve around Lorenzo, there are a number of clues to signal that his is not the most important, or only, story. First, the introductory description given of Lorenzo likens him to Hitler, already an indication that he will not be the most appealing of protagonists. Furthermore, the chapter heading consists of one word, *Amanda;* there is no mention of Lorenzo. The woman whose namesake entitles the chapter does not appear for several pages, most of which are focalized through Lorenzo, thus making the reader privy to both his desires and duplicity. Once on the scene, though, Amanda Scarlet determines the course of the events insofar as she dominates the thoughts and schemes of Lorenzo.

If these clues are indications that Lorenzo's person does not have primacy, the epigraph of the novel on the preceding page is even more suggestive. The epigraph consists of two definitions of *calypso.* The first identifies it as a song sung by slaves to recount the day's events and the abuses of the master. The second referent is Calypso, the woman in Homer's *Odyssey* on whose island Odysseus remained for seven years before returning to Penelope.

Like the cover illustration of *Entre Dios y el diablo,* its epigraph suggests a possible interpretation of the text that follows. Just as the master figures prominently in the calypsos of the slaves, so does Lorenzo occupy a central place in this narrative. Because of his will to power and machinations to preserve and increase it, the story concerns him. However, it is also as much the story of the Scarlet women, their history, and the influences of their world upon Lorenzo.

Capitalist par excellence, Lorenzo arrives in Parima Bay determined to make his fortune, and he uses all strategies at his disposal to attain this end. Lobo carefully constructs his figure not only to problematize the glory of progress but also to mock the justificatory discourse that affords it ideological support. Here the polyphony of the text is central because it shows the responses of the community's inhabitants as a counterpoint to the schemes of Lorenzo. In juxtaposing two or more interpretations of reality, the text discredits Lorenzo's discourse, which, like the rhetoric of imperial Europe, claims universality and supremacy.

Consider the explanation Lorenzo develops to justify his betrayal of Plantintáh and aspirations to marry Amanda Scarlet. Significantly, the elaboration of his argument occurs just as Lorenzo has discovered that capitalism is his raison d'être:

> Lorenzo manejaba, ahora, un lenguaje técnico y su pensamiento se estructuraba, cuadriculadamente, en ordenadas columnas. Si alguna vez se sintió inseguro, ya no lo estaba. Sabía perfectamente lo que quería de la vida, la duda no tenía cabida en sus propósitos. Es más, llegó a la conclusión de que Plantintáh Robinson había intentado aprovecharse de su buena fe, para explotar su capacidad de trabajo y su inteligencia. "Ese negro desgraciado—se decía—, quiso vivir a mis costillas." (37) [Lorenzo now had at his disposal a technical language, and his thoughts were structured neatly in ordered columns. If at any time he had felt insecure, he no longer did. He knew perfectly well what he wanted in life; there was no room for doubt in his purposes. What is more, he came to the conclusion that Plantintáh Robinson had tried to take advantage of his good faith, to exploit his capacity for work and his intelligence. "That miserable black man," he told himself, "wanted to live by the sweat of my brow."]

Here we see the construction of Lorenzo's colonialist "regime of truth," to abuse Bhabha's phrase (67). According to his own representation, Lorenzo denies that he has exploited Plantintáh, who interestingly enough loses his identity and becomes known simply by racial markers: "ese negro desgraciado." Lorenzo twists historical events—the joint establishment of the store and Lorenzo's subsequent solitary proprietorship—to legitimate his desires. From a guilty conscience, Lorenzo fashions a stereotype: Plantintáh is a black man who attempted to take advantage of the white man's industriousness in order to live at his expense.

This segment of text is especially interesting in light of Bhabha's analysis of the stereotype in colonial discourse. Bhabha has posited that "the stereotype is a complex, ambivalent, contradictory mode of representation, as anxious as it is assertive" (70). Though he is considering the deployment of the stereotype in colonial discourse, his comments are applicable to the historical situation fictionalized by *Calypso*, which recounts internal colonization within the modern state. The discourse of modernization and progress espoused by Lorenzo shares the same ends as colonial discourse as it is described by Bhabha: "The objective of colonial discourse is to construe the colonized as a population of degenerate types on the basis of racial origin, in order to justify conquest and to establish systems of administration and instruction" (70). Once Lorenzo finds himself in a position of power, he manipulates the representation of himself and others to rationalize his goals of personal enrichment and sexual gratification at the expense of the men and women of Parima Bay.

The obsessive sexual desires of Lorenzo can be considered in light of the theories of colonial desire elaborated by Robert J. C. Young. Lorenzo's disdain for the black man exists concurrently with his desire for the black woman. In fact, according to the novel, that desire is precisely what fuels Lorenzo's hatred of Plantintáh, whom he identifies as a rival. However, to categorize Plantintáh as a rival would place Plantintáh on equal terms, something Lorenzo cannot allow himself to imagine. Consider the following passage about Lorenzo: "Su envidia y sus celos los reducía a dos frases: una, la risa abunda en la boca de los tontos. La otra, Plantintáh no tenía huevos. De donde concluía, lapidariamente, que un tonto sin huevos no era un rival, así que muy pronto la misma Amanda acabaría por despreciarlo. Entonces aquí entraría él, Lorenzo" (31) [He reduced his envy and his jealousy to two phrases: one, laughter abounds in the mouths of fools. The other, Plantintáh has no balls. From whence he concluded tersely that a fool without balls was no rival, so very soon Amanda herself would end up scorning him. Here, then, Lorenzo himself would enter].

Again, as Bhabha notes, the "construction of the colonial subject in discourse, and the exercise of colonial power through discourse, demands an articulation of forms of difference—racial and sexual" (67). While Lorenzo can appreciate Amanda's esteem for Plantintáh, he cannot comprehend the latter's effusive fondness for Amanda, from which he concludes that Plantintáh is less than a man. This logic is entirely the product of Lorenzo's frustrated desire. Through the figure of Lorenzo, then, Lobo strips bare the grandiose discourse of civilization and progress, revealing petty personal motivations and risible myths of self-justification.

Though both Lorenzo and the Scarlet women play prominent roles, *Calypso* has no readily identifiable human protagonist. Rather, the novel is the tale of Parima Bay, the history of its inception and transformations. As such, it is the story of cultural exchange and interdependence in an increasingly globalized world. The three generations of Scarlet women—Amanda, Eudora, and Matilda—share the same time and space as Lorenzo Parima, but they belong to another circle of understanding that he finds incomprehensible. For instance, he cannot fathom the reasons for Amanda's refusal of marriage. He is just as startled by Eudora's acceptance for reasons of convenience. Unable to consummate the marriage with Eudora because of his impotence, Lorenzo turns his frustrated energies to business endeavors, leaving his wife to engage in multiple affairs behind his back.

As seen in his marriage to Eudora, Lorenzo needs the community more than Parima Bay needs him. Even though the town carries his name, it is clear from the story that it is Lorenzo's identity that is determined by the community and not the reverse. He notes, "El pueblo no parecía necesitarlo. En cambio él, sí" (206) [The town did not seem to need him. He, though, did]. He returns twice to the capital, and each time feels out of place, unable to recognize the place of his birth or his own brother. On his first trip, he checks out of the fine hotel where he had sought lodging and moves to a small place populated mostly by blacks because he feels more comfortable among them. His sense of self depends on his relationship to Parima Bay; there he is certain of his racial and social identity.

In contrast, the community has an identity apart from the man who gave it a name and economic organization. As the story progresses, it becomes clear that Lorenzo is less the center than the dependent and that every effort he takes to exert more control results in his inevitable frustration. There is a rhythm of life in the community that he cannot dominate. The African preaches against envy, Eudora blackmails him, Miss Emily taunts him, Stella thwarts his efforts at multiple turns. The oral culture of the people, rich in mocking laughter and pointed stories, humiliates and defeats Lorenzo in his moments of greatest aspiration. Like the trickster Anansi, in the African tales spun by the local storyteller, el Jamaiquino, the people of Parima Bay are adept at evading the efforts of those more powerful than they.

Even the modernization that comes to Parima Bay as a result of Lorenzo's development is transformed into something else by the community. Lobo humorously fictionalizes processes of cultural reconversion, affirming the ability of marginalized cultures not only to retain their identities but to adapt new knowledge to their situations. This is particularly evident when Stella attempts to communicate with her ancestors. Repeating the Latin names of butterflies recorded carefully by a long-departed entomologist, Stella dances in an effort to commune with her forebears:

> De modo que cuando la albina intentaba comunicarse con sus ancestros, entre bastones pintados, flores secas y caracolas de mar, lo que en realidad hacía era invocar a las mariposas más bellas . . . con una letanía hipnótica y cadenciosa que sonaba como un canto gregoriano en la alucinante atmósfera nocturna de la selva tropical. . . . Entonces, desde el bastón central, un resplandor de plata se extendía. . . . Stella nunca las vio porque mantenía los ojos cerrados y confundía sus

lentos aleteos con el susurro de sus antepasados, y su roce con las caricias de sus abuelos. (137) [So when the albino, surrounded by painted staffs, dried flowers, and sea shells, tried to communicate with her ancestors, what she was really doing was invoking the most beautiful butterflies . . . with a hypnotic, cadenced litany that sounded like a Gregorian chant in the hallucinatory, nocturnal atmosphere of the tropical forest. . . . Then, from the central staff, a silver gleam shone forth. . . . Stella never saw the butterflies because she kept her eyes shut, and she mistook the slow fluttering of their wings for the murmuring of her ancestors, and their brushing against her for the caresses of her grandparents.]

Introducing Latin names into a new environment ("la selva tropical") and the rites of Afro-Latin American religious practices ("bastones pintados" and "caracolas de mar"), Stella appropriates and transforms these signs for her own purposes. The passage is a remarkable allegory for cultural reconversion.

In fact, the entire novel is an appropriation and reconversion of other discourses and cultures. A fundamentally intertextual work, it draws upon a multitude of texts and traditions that it mocks, parodies, and deconstructs in its pages. Humor is central to this process in the novel. Subversive laughter introduces disorder, shatters illusions, points out inconsistencies. Lobo's humor is parodic humor, which Arias defines as not being "la risa catártica aristotélica, sino más bien la risa carnavalizante bajtiniana que escapa al control de poder vigente, ideológico o literario, adquiriendo el vigor de la denuncia, rompiendo la ilusión y cuestionando los valores tradicionales. . . . La parodia es el perfecto vehículo para escenificar ideologías sin aparecer ideológico a su vez" ("Descolonizando," 83) [cathartic Aristotelian laughter, but rather carnivalizing Bakhtinian laughter that escapes the control of the prevailing ideological or literary powers and acquires the strength of a denouncement, shattering illusion and questioning traditional values. . . . Parody is the perfect vehicle to dramatize ideologies without appearing ideological oneself]. Just as the plot is the story of the limitations of the "poder vigente" in the face of the Bakhtinian laughter of community residents, the novel as a whole is a problematization of contemporary coloniality, cast now in terms of global markets.

The deconstructive representation of history is also an intertextual enterprise that exists in dialogue with the rhetoric of the modern, progressive welfare state that is Costa Rica, or at least Costa Rica as promulgated by políticos and consumed by ecotourists and World Bank officials. It is useful to remember that the last half-century is the time in which the image of the country as the Switzerland of Central America was carefully constructed and exported. For Costa Rica, the image was a triumph of modernism, which according to Néstor García Canclini's definition is a process in which "elites take charge of the intersection of different historical temporalities and try to elaborate a global project with them" (46). The most recent global project revolves around neoliberalism and consumer culture. In the face of this, *Calypso* reclaims heterogeneity and contradictions in Costa Rican society, showing the "sedimentation, juxtaposition, and interweaving" of multiple traditions and temporalities (46).

In the process of reclaiming heterogeneities, the text appropriates, dismantles, and inverts the favorite tropes and plots of Boom narrative. The novel is a contestatory representation of these works. It actively engages the discourse of the Spanish-American literary masters and calculates a response. In doing so, it questions their representations, self-conscious innovations, and aspirations to grandeur.

For instance, though Boom narratives challenged Latin American history and politics through fiction, they frequently reiterated the same gender and ethnic biases as the system they criticized. As Pellón notes, recent Spanish American narrative shares a tendency to retell the stories of the Boom from other angles: "the perspective of more marginal elements of society increasingly comes to the fore" (280). The post-Boom novels "capture, not the voices of mythified *caudillos,* or alienated intellectuals, but the voices of those who for social, economic, and historical reasons have been silenced" (281). Authors after the Boom draw upon the wealth of narrative innovation of their predecessors to tell other stories.

An excellent example of Lobo's appropriation of the master's discourse of the Boom is the last scene of *Calypso*. The scene also highlights the limitations of globalized coloniality in imposing a new cultural and economic system. The last pages of the novel show Stella's increasingly desperate attempts to console Matilda's cousin Omfí. Omfí is disconsolate after the death of Matilda and her boyfriend at the hands of Lorenzo's thugs. The young couple died as they attempted to raid a shipment of illegal goods, supposedly electronic items but actually huge quantities of cocaine Lorenzo had been trafficking. Stella takes Omfí to the abandoned ritual site in the woods and begins to dance, and "entonces la tierra se encabritó como una yegua en celo" (264) [then the earth reared up like a mare in heat]. The whole town flees to the *cerrito de los olvidos* [hill of forgetting] to avoid the impending tidal wave that washes over Parima Bay. In its wake, the inhabitants look over the town:

Al replegarse el agua, los asombrados pariminos vieron cómo el comisariato, socavados sus podridos basamentos, caía, desmoronándose, con una terrible crujidera de vigas desgajadas. . . . lo que hasta ese momento había sido el centro de la vida del pueblo fue un polvazal que se desprendió cubriendo con una mancha marrón el trozo de la playa. . . . En ese momento, la gente comprendió que el nombre del pueblo ya no tenía sentido puesto que el rótulo que le había dado identidad desaparecía, aplastado, bajo el óxido de viejas latas de zinc. (265–66) [When the water withdrew, the astonished Paraminos watched how the commissary, its rotten foundation undermined, fell crumbling with a terrible grinding of broken beams. . . . what had until this moment been the center of the life of the town was a dust heap that fell apart, covering a section of beach with a brown stain. At that moment, the people understood that the name of the town no longer made sense, now that the sign that had given it its identity had disappeared, crushed beneath the rust of old tin cans.]

Lorenzo's inscription perishes in the wake of Stella's performance. As a result, the Paraminos realize the arbitrariness of the identity they had previously accepted without question. Faced with the collapse of the symbolic center of town, the manipulated and marginalized inhabitants understand that they have an existence that does not depend on Lorenzo or his business.

The conclusion of *Calypso* contains ironic echoes of *Cien años de soledad*, the most famous fictionalized history of Latin America. As in *Cien años*, the end is ushered in by a cataclysmic natural event of supernatural proportions. In *Cien años*, this turns Macondo into a dusty whirlwind. Rather than the dusty wind of forgetfulness, in *Calypso* it is the crushing power of water that sweeps over the city. Unlike the dust of Macondo, the water of Parima Bay does not symbolize death and sterility but regeneration for the community.

Additionally, Lobo locates her protagonist outside the symbolic space of privilege occupied in *Cien años* by Aureliano, who reads and perishes simultaneously. In marked contrast to both Aureliano and Lorenzo's store, the people of Parima Bay survive because they do not occupy the center. They are geographically positioned at the periphery, standing on the hill and observing the destruction below. For this reason, in *Calypso* the tidal wave does not represent the end simply because it collapses the commissary and drives Lorenzo from town once and for all. Rather, the human community persists with or without its name and patron, respectfully refusing to burn the remnants of the store until Lorenzo comes to do it himself. Unlike the history of Macondo, the history of Parima Bay cannot be erased because it is performed, not written. It does not follow a predetermined script, but rather takes shape in the stories and dances of the Stellas of the world. The history of Parima Bay is negotiated and acted out; it evolves over time, reflecting and contributing to the reality around it.

The last line of *Calypso*, which describes Matilda's dancing, is particularly significant: "Antífona y respuesta, baila sobre los escombros" (267) [Antiphony and response, she dances on the debris]. The phantom dancing on the ruined store represents the symbolic defeat of Lorenzo, who flees to his contemporary Penelope, a madam who offers stability and economic advancement. The myth of Matilda's presence also represents an attempt by the people of Parima Bay to convert their loss into a legacy of resilience and triumph, in which Matilda, like Stella, counters the melancholy of the inhabitants with a dance.

Like that of *Asalto al paraíso,* the conclusion is ambiguous. In both novels, a performance undoes an inscription, symbolizing the failure of hegemonic, lettered culture to control completely those it marginalizes. Stella's dance trumps Lorenzo's writing; Pedro's opening of the gate reverses endless decrees he penned as a scribe to legitimate the war on Talamanca. In both novels, though, the symbols of the old order disappear. Store, black rooster, and two generations of Scarlet women are taken by the ocean in the last pages of *Calypso.* In *Asalto,* Presbere dies and Talamanca goes up in flames. However, from the destruction rise new myths: that Matilda dances, Pedro lives, Presbere's spirit persists among the guacamayas. Though the victories are pyrrhic, Lobo's projects affirm the capacity of marginalized groups to offer a counterpoint in the colony and the new world order.

In a Globalized World

Along with Belli's *Waslala, Calypso* brings the topics of globalization to the pages of Central American fiction, making it an appropriate conclusion to the present study. Both published in the same year, the fictions explore the dynamics and implications of narcotrafficking and neocolonial exploitation, two forms of capitalist enterprise that sacrifice lives in the pursuit of prosperity. The novels not only recover the history of women and subalterns, they also locate the region in a larger system of cultural and economic exchange. And ultimately they introduce the reader to new forms of violence and social injustice in Central America.

In *Calypso,* Lobo stops short of affirming a definitive victory for women and subalterns, just as Belli does in her fiction. Though her ghost dances, Matilda is still dead while Lorenzo lives punished only by his guilty conscience. Similarly, though the affirmed and renewed Melisandra sets out running from Waslala, the destruction of the people and land of Faguas continues.

Significantly, though, both Belli and Lobo link cultural expressions to resistance from alternative centers of power. In *Calypso,* it is Stella's dance, inherited from Miss Emily, that ends Lorenzo's interference in Parima Bay. In *Waslala,* poetry inspires the determination to reclaim Faguas. There are no definitive victories for either author, nor are there resounding defeats. Lavinia perishes, Talamanca burns, Lorenzo lives, but Belli and Lobo imply a continuing legacy of subversion, appropriation, and persistence manifested across generations. Rather than a dialectic concluding in synthesis, the stories posit a dynamic vision of culture. Like Lobo, each one of the women writers included here imagines the world divorced from binaries, where culture is contested and all retain traces of those Others with whom they interact.

Conclusion

Where Now?

History and the Present

[T]hose texts which open up to the multiple and often antagonistic discourses of the continent represent a political as well as an aesthetic choice, a Utopia glimpsed beyond the nightmare of an as yet unfinished modernity.

—Jean Franco, "The Nation as Imagined Community"

WHEN ALEGRÍA, BELLI, Aguilar, and Lobo fictionalize historical events in their novels, they write for the present and the future. They signal the need for modern societies to come to terms with the past. And their texts, which embrace "multiple and antagonistic discourses," represent political and aesthetic choices that gesture toward utopias beyond the present distress.

The authors' individual confrontations with coloniality and modernity in Central America lead them to question history. If the past is as it has been represented, they ask, why does the present look like it does? There are two possibilities: either the present is being misinterpreted or the past has been misrepresented. Faced with injustice, war, and violence, they dismiss the first possibility and investigate the latter.

Their historical fiction is one response to events that brought repressed histories to the front page. The writers began to speak out at a critical moment when the hegemonic powers (namely, the government and the economic elite) lost their ability to persuade and turned to violence to maintain social order. Throughout the 1970s and 1980s the Nicaraguan revolution, civil war in El Salvador, and genocide in Guatemala showed that modern life and political participation were unattainable dreams for many. Censorship and brutal repression also revealed that the imposition of national unity came at a great human cost.

The buried past moved once again to the surface in the 1990s, which is when the last of the group of writers, Tatiana Lobo, began to publish her historical fiction. The protests organized to commemorate the quincentennial of Columbus's voyage, the 1992 awarding of the Nobel Peace Prize to Rigoberta Menchú, and the Zapatista uprising concurrent with the implementation of NAFTA, all reinforced the image that modernity was at best "unfinished" for many people.

The exposure of the myths that maintained national order is the common cultural denominator in the Central American crises, the quincentennial protests, and popular challenges to the ruling class in Mexico. The decades of civil turmoil, followed by the magnetic pull of the forces of globalization, have exposed a core of contradictions in Latin American culture and society. Art and literature contemporaneous with the period often reveal the fissures, hypocrisies, and problems of the nations. Mobilized by Others, often for the first time, this literary discourse has a dual purpose: to demythologize the establishment and to posit an alternative social arrangement. The historical fictions of Alegría, Belli, Aguilar, and Lobo, like other critiques, challenge interpretations of the past, especially those mobilized to justify the status quo.

Born in the midst of national disintegration, the novels probe the silences and tensions concealed in dominant narratives about the past. In their supplements to the story of modernity, Alegría, Belli,

Aguilar, and Lobo critique the past in light of modern concerns. And in their interest in recovering women's history, they share much in common with postcolonial writers from Africa, India, and the Caribbean, who also reconfigure notions of memory and identity in the new world order. Postcolonial writers, as Helen Tiffin points out,

> have from the outset been attempting to establish or rehabilitate self against either European appropriation or rejection. Because postcolonial and colonial perspectives are necessarily informed by the imperial vision with which they are always in various ways and to varying degrees implicated, such establishing or rehabilitation of an independent identity involves the radical interrogation and fracturing of these imposed European perspectives, and their ... replacement by an alternative vision. (172)

In their "radical interrogation and fracturing" of identities, the Central American authors suggest that these identities are the result of a colonial *and* patriarchal legacy. They respond to the colonization of not only territories and peoples but also of women and their memories. They confront women's own status as colonial subjects whose bodies and histories must be reclaimed to create a space of resistance. In doing so, they reassess the "foundational fictions" that explain the nation and the roles of men *and* women that comprise it.

Using the "counterculture of the imagination," Alegría, Belli, Aguilar, and Lobo challenge the utopias of Latin America brokered to the wealthy and powerful (Tiffin, 176). According to Tiffin, the counterculture of the imagination "promotes polyphony, eschews fixity, monocentrism and closure, interrogates concepts such as history and textuality, [and] opposes oral to written formulations ... by inhabiting the absences or oppositional 'positions' in the imperial textual record, and from these absences or oppositions interrogating its presence or fixity" (176). Writers who use these strategies "seek to recast history as a 'redefinable present rather than an irrevocably interpreted past'" (176). Subversive strategies like those Tiffin describes abound in the texts of Alegría, Belli, Aguilar, and Lobo. Each author fictionalizes history, "inhabiting absences" in the historical record of both empire and nation. In their counterculture of the imagination, they bring women to the foreground, especially during specific moments of crisis or transition in Central America. And as their texts bring into focus the absence of women from historical record, they show the limits of its interpretive lens. Since no record exists for most women, the authors imagine the history of those who never appeared as subjects in their own right.

Their stories also trouble boundaries between genres, showing the similarities between historical and fictional narratives. They point out the constructed nature of history, which in turn opens the door for the consideration of women's history and a questioning of historiography in general. This is an important contribution in Latin America, for as Carmen Ramos has observed, "The awareness of the importance of women's history is a relatively recent phenomenon and in Latin America has been mainly confined to research institutions and to organised groups of women interested in finding out about their past. Today's task is to break away from the long-held notion of history as a mere catalogue of political events and to change to a more modern, active conception of it as a collective interpretation of the past in which women have a relevant part to play" (318). The writers I have considered take their stories to a public beyond institutions and universities. They thus multiply the impact of academic discussions among a broader audience.

As they engage the historical record, Alegría, Belli, Aguilar, and Lobo demystify and demythologize it. They also radically challenge modern structures that have found their legitimation in the traditions they dismantle. According to liberalism and neoliberalism, the story of modern nations is a plot with readily identifiable characters. It involves nations, guided by leaders, in steady progress toward "civilization" and prominence. However, as with any story, it is easy to grasp the plot, more difficult to understand its nuances. Explaining the silences, biases, and inconsistencies in the story exposes traditional representations of the past as contingent interpretations. It emphasizes the interdependence of history and ideological programs. And it means coming to terms with the absence of women and others.

The fictionalized histories of Alegría, Belli, Aguilar, and Lobo thus become dangerous supplements to a record that long claimed supremacy. Ultimately, the authors do not just challenge the emplotment of past events. They challenge present identities dependent on a particular rendering of history. In short, their stories are political and aesthetic acts, gesturing toward utopia. The past is not what it was, they suggest, and neither is the future. Again, there are other plots in Central America.

Appendix

Central American Women Writers

A Bibliographical Survey

CENTRAL AMERICAN TEXTS offer a fascinating range of ideas and stories, but they do not usually achieve the circulation of their Mexican, Cuban, or Southern Cone peers. Most of the neglect is due to economic factors rather than literary merit. Central American publishing houses have limited funds and small domestic markets. Only late in the 1990s did international publishing houses like Alfaguara and Farben begin producing significant numbers of Central American texts. Although it is by no means exhaustive, I offer the following survey of women's texts from the region as an introduction and resource for the interested reader.

For generalists and specialists alike, the existence (since 1993) of an international conference on Central American literature, the Congreso Internacional de Literatura Centroamericana (CILCA), has provided a forum for critical exchanges on texts. It has been organized through Purdue University–Calumet and was founded by Jorge Román-Lagunas of that institution. It covers a wide range of topics, and gender-related presentations have increased in popularity each year. In 1999, for example, there were six panels dedicated to literature and gender. The conference has also provided an outlet for the distribution of books and materials in a region that has long depended on informal mechanisms of cultural exchange.

The World Wide Web also features a number of pages dedicated to Central American writers. Sometimes listed by author names (www.sergioramirez.com, for example) or through institutions, these sites have facilitated publication and exchange among authors, critics, and students of the literature worldwide.

For English-language publications, readers may consult booklists by Curbstone Press. This not-for-profit foundation has published English translations of Claribel Alegría, Tatiana Lobo, Rosario Aguilar, and others from Central America. Spanish-language presses are often country specific, and some are no longer in business. In Nicaragua, presses founded under the Sandinista government saw their funding shrink or disappear after 1990, and several went bankrupt. Nevertheless, notable presses include Anamá (with which Gioconda Belli is associated), Nueva Nicaragua, Vanguardia, and Decenio. In Costa Rica, Editorial Mujeres was headed by Linda Berrón during the 1990s but was reportedly defunct by the time of writing. The Editorial de la Universidad de Costa Rica also has published women's writing and criticism, as has the private Colombia-based press Farben. In Honduras, the Editorial Guardabarranca and Editorial Guaymuras are notable for their publications of texts by women. In El Salvador, the Ministry of Culture seems to be the principal outlet for publication, along with university presses. The same is true for Guatemala, where the Ministry of Culture publishes a number of texts. Artemis and Edinter is another publishing house active in Guatemala. Regionally, EDUCA, the Editorial Universitaria Centroamericana, is an important press. It is comprised of a consortium of prominent universities and distributes the most comprehensive range of titles.

Women's Texts by Country

It is a logical consequence that as more Central America women write and publish, they introduce new voices in literary and cultural circles and also articulate concerns previously unspoken either in fiction or in public debates. For instance, many women began to elaborate a woman-centered erotic beginning in the 1970s, while others introduced the question of gender into discussions of politics and history. In the following country-by-country survey, I attempt to identify major writers and their works, as well as some of the themes they have broached.

Testimonial Literature

Testimonial literature of Central America was among the first genres to facilitate the entry of women's voices into contemporary dialogues and debates. The bibliography on testimonial literature is abundant, and I refer readers to John Beverley and Marc Zimmerman's *Literature and Politics in the Central American Revolutions* (1990) for a good introduction to the subject. Also useful is Beverley's *Against Literature* (1993). *Me llamo Rigoberta Menchú y así me nació la conciencia* (1984), related by Rigoberta Menchú to Elisabeth Burgos-Debray, is the most prominent (and controversial) testimony from Central America. For more on the debate, see *The Rigoberta Menchú Controversy*, edited by Arturo Arias (2001).

El Salvador

Claribel Alegría (b. 1924) is arguably the most familiar author in Central American letters. Her first novel, *Cenizas de Izalco* (1966), was published with her husband and was a finalist in the Biblioteca Breve competition sponsored by Seix Barral, and her poetry has received critical acclaim as well. She has remained active into her seventies and she completed a reading tour with renowned poet Ernesto Cardenal in the northeastern United States in 2002. With forty books published, Alegría has few peers among women writers in the region. Certainly in El Salvador there has been none with a comparable reputation since the death of poet Claudia Lars (1899–1974), who wrote *Canción redonda* (1937) and *La casa de vidrio* (1942). A number of younger Salvadoran women have begun to publish poetry, short stories, and novels. Among them, Jacinta Escudos (b. 1961), is a rising author of narrative. Among Escudos's works are *Apuntes de una historia de amor que no fue* (1987), *El desencanto* (2001), and *Felicidad doméstica y otras cosas aterradoras* (2002), the last a collection of narratives with family as a central theme. For a critical perspective on women artists, see the Concultura report "Mujeres artistas en El Salvador: Diagnóstico" (1998), produced by María Luisa Angulo, which analyzes the problems and achievements of women artists in the country.

Nicaragua

In Nicaragua, Rosario Aguilar (b. 1938) and Gioconda Belli (b. 1948) are the most renowned women novelists, and each has had multiple editions as well as translations of works published. In a country recognized more for its poetic tradition than its narrative, the authors have gained a degree of recognition unprecedented for a woman writer. After having reached celebrity status during the Sandinista period, Belli in particular remains a popular figure in Nicaragua. She began writing poetry during the 1970s, the earliest of which appeared in *Sobre la grama* (1974). She has also authored three novels: *La mujer habitada* (1988), *Sofía de los presagios* (1992), and *Waslala*

(1996). Her most recent volume of poetry, *Apogeo* (1997) incorporates new imagery while retaining the defiant voice for which she became known. Her memoirs, entitled *El país bajo mi piel* (2001), recount the personal contours of her life as they have been shaped by political realities. The English-language version, *The Country under My Skin* (2002), received considerable press coverage in U.S. media outlets. Though she resides in California, Belli currently is involved in the Managua-based Anamá Press, which has published her own work as well as that of other writers.

Aguilar is author of numerous texts in narrative. She wrote her first novel, *Primavera sonámbula* (1964), in her twenties, and has continued to publish regularly since. She is also author of *Quince barrotes de izquierda a derecha* (1965), *Rosa Sarmiento* (1968), *Aquel mar sin fondo ni playa* (1970), *Las doce y veintinueve* (1975), and *El guerrillero* (1976), all of which have been republished in the three-volume *Colección primavera sonámbula* (1999). *Siete relatos sobre el amor y la guerra* (1986), and *La niña blanca y los pájaros sin pies* (1992) are two more recent novels. In 1999 Aguilar was inducted into the Academia Nicaragüense de la Lengua, an unprecedented occurrence since the institution had been exclusively male since its founding.

Several women poets found a forum within Sandinismo in the 1970s and 1980s. Along with Belli, Vidaluz Meneses (b. 1944), Daisy Zamora (b. 1950), and Michele Najlis (b. 1946) all made important contributions to the poetic tradition associated with the revolution. Prominent publications include Najlis's *El viento armado* (1969) and Zamora's *La violenta espuma* (1981), a collection of poems written between 1968 and 1978. Ana Ilce Gómez (b. 1945) also published *Las ceremonias del silencio* (1975) during the period of the Sandinista struggle, though her writing is less overtly political than that of the others.

In general, postrevolutionary poetry reflects the transition in Nicaragua after the 1990 electoral defeat of the Sandinistas, articulating a more intimate world, less infused with overtly political imagery.

Significant poetic texts published after the revolution include *Llama en el aire* by Meneses (1991), Najlis's *Cantos de Ifigenia* (1991), and Zamora's *A cada quien la vida* (1994). Blanca Castellón (b. 1958) began her writing career in the post-Sandinista years with poems similar to haikus in their brevity and their ability to evoke images. In *Ama del espíritu* (1995), her succinct style transforms observations of the quotidian into revelations.

Costa Rica

Unlike Nicaragua, Costa Rica has a much longer tradition of women in narrative, particularly in the novel and short story. The work of Yolanda Oreamuno (1916–1956) remained neglected until fairly recently; Costa Rican society commented more on her beauty than her literary talents within her own lifetime. Lately, however, her complex psychological novel *La ruta de su evasión* (1949) has begun to receive critical attention. Oreamuno's contemporary and friend Eunice Odio (1922–1974) wrote similarly sophisticated pieces in poetry. Her works include *El tránsito de fuego* (1957) and *Territorio del alba* (1974), a collection she was assembling before her death. Like Oreamuno, she too remained virtually unknown in her own country for many years.

By contrast, subsequent decades saw Carmen Naranjo (b. 1928) become a very visible figure in her capacity as a diplomat, minister, and publishing company director. Naranjo also wrote narrative works, including the novel *Los perros no ladraron* (1966) and the short story collection *Ondina* (1982). Linda Berrón (b. 1951) has attained similar stature, directing the Editorial Mujeres until its demise and publishing in several genres. Her projects include the novel *El expediente* (1989) and the drama *Olimpia* (1997). Ana Istarú (b. 1960) is author of both drama and poetry, and her take on maternity in *Baby Boom en el paraíso* (2001; performed 1996) has played before audiences in Spain, Costa Rica, and most recently Chicago. Novelist Anacristina

Rossi (b. 1952) enjoyed a smashing success with *La loca de Gandoca* (1992), which sold more than forty thousand copies and introduced readers to a new ecological focus in fiction. Rossi's *Limón Blues* (2002), the first part of a trilogy, depicts the frequently overlooked Afro-Caribbean communities of the Atlantic coast of Costa Rica. The Atlantic coast is also the focus of *La flota negra* (1999) by Yazmín Ross (b. 1959). Ross also collaborated with Luciano Capelli on a documentary film about Marcus Garvey, the black activist who spent time in Costa Rica. Nicaraguan-born Irma Prego (1933–2000), author of *Mensajes al más allá,* also wrote and published in Costa Rica prior to her death. U.S.-based Costa Rican writer Rima de Vallbona (b. 1931), has several publications, including her highly successful first work, *Noche en vela* (1968). Other Costa Rican women writers include Carmen Lyra (1888–1949), writer of both children's stories and literature for adults, and Julieta Pinto (b. 1922), winner of national literary prizes and author of several titles.

Though Costa Rica did not experience its own social revolution, it did feel the effects of these in the region, harboring exiles and receiving a flood of legal and illegal immigrants. On this and other topics, Costa Rican women writers have made pointed social commentary in fiction, focusing especially on the politics of familial and social structures. Examples par excellence of this are the short stories "Una mujer llamada Carmela" by Prego, "Encuentro simbiótico" by Naranjo, and Berrón's novel *El expediente* (1989), each of which explores the nature of gender relationships. Vallbona also makes mordant observations of the family in *Noche en vela,* as well as in her subsequent narrative works published in both Costa Rica and the United States. Appearing on the literary stage with her 1990 publication of *Tiempo de claveles,* Tatiana Lobo (b. 1939) has made several provocative contributions to Costa Rican literature, including a collection of short stories, three novels, and a historical work on race entitled *Negros y blancos: Todo mezclado* (1997), produced in collaboration with genealogist Mauricio Meléndez.

Guatemala

In comparison to other countries, Guatemala does not have such an established tradition of women narrators, except in the testimonial genre. A notable exception is Isabel Garma (1940–1998), who published the book of short stories *El hoyito de perraje* (1994) and other works. Among gifted Guatemalan poets are numerous women writers, including Luz Méndez de la Vega (b. 1919). Ana María Rodas (b. 1937) is perhaps the best known and is author of *Poemas de la izquierda erótica* (1973) and *El fin de los mitos y los sueños* (1984). Aída Toledo (b. 1952) has also been active in poetry, publishing in the 1990s works like *Realidad más extraña que el sueño* (1994). Her compatriot Mildred Hernández (b. 1966) has published two narrative works, *Orígenes* (1995), a collection of short stories, and *Diario de cuerpos* (1998).

Honduras

In Honduras, Lucila Gamero de Medina (1873–1964) wrote her novel *Blanca Olmedo* (1903) long before women's writing enjoyed the forum it has today. In poetry the most well known Honduran woman writer is Clementina Suárez (1903–1991), who began to publish in the 1930s and continued to be active until her murder in 1991. *Creciendo con la hierba* (1957) and *Con mis versos saludo a las generaciones futuras* (1988) are two of her works.

Contemporary poets include Aída Ondina Sabonge (b. 1958), who in *Declaración doméstica* (1993) blends social consciousness with reflections on her role as a woman. Other authors of her generation publish their poetry in literary magazines and books. For instance, in the 1990s, poet Amanda Castro (b. 1962) of Honduras used these forums to probe the limitations and injustices faced by women. The work of this younger generation of Honduran poets has also found an outlet in literary journals as well as in publications by Editorial Guardabarranca and Editorial Guaymuras.

Anthologies and Critical Studies

The 1990s saw the publication in Central America of national anthologies of women's writing. In Nicaragua, Daisy Zamora's *Mujer nicaragüense en la poesía* (1992) is notable. In Costa Rica, Linda Berrón published *Relatos de mujeres* (1993), an anthology of narrative by Costa Rican women writers. Aída Toledo and Anabella Acevedo Leal produced *Tanta imagen tras la puerta* (1999), an anthology of poetry by Guatemalan women. For Honduras, Adaluz Pineda de Gálvez has collected the poetry of women in *Honduras, mujer y poesía* (1998). The latter grew out of the short-lived Grupo Cultural Femenino "Clementina Suárez" in Tegucigalpa and was published by Editorial Guardabarranco. Also, poet Amanda Castro has included the work of more than fifteen women writers in the bilingual anthology *Poetry by Contemporary Honduran Women* (2002).

University women have also published a number of critical essays on women and culture. Helen Umaña of Honduras has two collections of essays on contemporary authors and includes women in both. Yadira Calvo of Costa Rica is author of many titles, including *Literatura, mujer, y sexismo* (1984). United States–based critic Janet Gold published *Volver a imaginarlas: Retratos de escritoras centroamericanas* (1998) in Honduras. Eugenia Rodríguez Sáenz edited *Mujeres, género e historia en América Central* (2002), a text that considers gender issues over three centuries. While most of the essays are oriented more toward the social sciences, the volume does include works on literature and the arts. In a similar vein, there is Rodríguez's *Un siglo de luchas femeninas en América Latina* (2002), which contains a section devoted to gender studies in the university.

Other critical works from Central America include author-specific studies like Nidia Palacios's *Voces femeninas en la narrativa de Rosario Aguilar* (1998). On Costa Rican literature in general there is *Casa paterna* (1993). In this work, authors Flora Ovares, Margarita Rojas, Carlos Santander, and María Elena Carballo discuss Costa Rican literature from the perspective of feminism and theories of culture. Edited by Eugenia Rodríguez Sáenz, *Entre silencios y voces* (1997) also contains studies on gender and history in Central America from numerous scholars of the region. For a general perspective on Central American literature between 1960 and 1990, see Arturo Arias's *Gestos ceremoniales* (1998). There is also a monographic edition of Australian-based *Antípodas*, published as *De la guerra a la paz: Perspectivas críticas sobre la literatura moderna centroamericana* (2002) and edited by Ricardo Roque Baldovinos and Roy Boland Osegueda.

In the United States, a number of critics have worked consistently with texts by Central American women and numerous others who have published occasional pieces on writers from the region. Dedicated exclusively to the Honduran writer's work is Janet Gold's *Clementina Suárez: Her Life and Poetry* (1995). Gold also has a Spanish-language study of Clementina Suárez published in Honduras. Ileana Rodríguez has several articles on the region and addresses Central American women's writing in her books *House/Garden/Nation* (1994) and *Women, Guerrillas, and Love* (1996), both on broader topics in Latin American literature. Similarly, Linda Craft's *Novels of Testimony and Resistance from Central America* (1997) contains chapters relevant to women's writing, as well as useful background information on Central America. Among authors of articles Amy Kaminsky and Kathleen March figure prominently, having published several articles on Central American women writers. There are numerous others whose interest has been captured by one or more authors, and I refer the interested reader to the MLA database and on-line library indices for the most current information on critical studies.

Notes

Unless otherwise noted, all translations are mine.

Introduction

1. The phrase "dangerous supplement" is borrowed from Jacques Derrida. Derrida, in turn, has borrowed from Jean Jacques Rousseau. See chapter 2 in *Of Grammatology* (1976) for Derrida's understanding of the phrase.

2. *El güegüense* is a satirical drama first performed during the colonial period in Nicaragua. It showcases the code switching, double entendres, and other tactics used by the mestizo and Indian populations to mock colonial officials and thwart their plans. See David Whisnant's *Rascally Signs in Sacred Places* (1995, 28–29) and the introductory notes to Jorge Eduardo Arellano's edition of *El güegüense* (1998).

3. *Exteriorismo* was an approach to poetry advocated by Ernesto Cardenal. The exteriorist poem was ideally one expressed in clear and direct language, free from metaphor and simile, and committed to presenting reality. Pushed in poetry workshops after the Nicaraguan revolution, the movement came under harsh criticism from some artists and intellectuals who feared the imposition of a "cultural standard" associated with the revolution.

4. For an introduction to and overview of the Menchú controversy, see Arturo Arias, ed., *The Rigoberta Menchú Controversy* (2001).

5. Solentiname was a community organized by Cardenal on Mancarrón island in Lake Nicaragua in the late 1960s. An experiment grounded in Christian communism, Solentiname gathered the peasants who lived on Mancarrón together to forge a better existence and to raise revolutionary consciousness among them. Eventually, Solentiname became a center for primitivist art and attracted international attention. The community was destroyed in 1977 by the Nicaraguan national guard.

6. Unfortunately, there have been few studies dedicated to the literary production of Central America. John Beverley and Marc Zimmerman's *Literature and Politics in the Central American Revolutions* (1990) was a

seminal work, including a very valuable discussion of testimonial literature and the participation of women in that genre. *Novels of Testimony and Resistance from Central America* (1997) by Linda Craft offered a more contemporary view of the field, and she included chapters on Belli and Alegría, the most widely known women of the region. Ileana Rodríguez has also authored numerous articles on Central America. Her *Women, Guerrillas, and Love* (1996) is a study of war and literature in Central America that has taken gender concerns explicitly into consideration, though predominantly with an eye toward the revolutions of the past.

7. Feminist scholars rightly assert that the token insertion of such women into the record does not transform the system but rather reinforces it.

8. See Lerner's feminist classic, *The Majority Finds Its Past* (1979).

9. The Boom refers to the increased dissemination of Latin American texts in the 1960s and 1970s. Authors frequently associated with the Boom include Carlos Fuentes, Gabriel García Márquez, and Mario Vargas Llosa. García Márquez's *Cien años de soledad* (1967) is generally seen as the quintessential Boom novel.

10. In Central America in the 1970s and 1980s, decades-old dictatorial regimes, like those of Nicaragua (which fell in 1979) and El Salvador, were being challenged. In contrast, in Southern Cone countries, repressive governments were being founded. The 1973 coup in Chile ended a long democratic tradition in that country, and with American academic advisers, the subsequent Pinochet regime inaugurated neoliberal policies on a wide scale. Though the Mexican government was not a dictatorship, it was dominated by the corrupt, one-party government of the PRI (Partido Revolucionario Institucional; Institutional Revolutionary Party), which suffered electoral defeat at the presidential level for the first time in 2000.

11. Marxist critics would call these texts expressions of "bourgeois decadence."

12. The term "woman-centered" has been used by critics to refer to texts written by women and concerned with women's experiences, though the texts themselves may not be overtly feminist. The term "woman" in this context draws attention to gender, unlike the term "female," which suggests biology, and the term "feminist," which concerns ideology. Finally, it is important to note that in the wake of a general backlash against feminism since the 1970s, the term "woman" has gained currency as an inclusive and neutral term.

13. For more on the social consequences of free-market reforms, which often involve "austerity measures" to control inflation, see Paul Drake's *Money Doctors, Foreign Debts, and Economic Reforms in Latin America* (1994).

14. Though he was the indubitable center of modernism, Darío spent much of his life in Europe and in other Latin American countries.

Chapter 1

1. In El Salvador in the 1960s and 1970s, secular leftist organizations and radical Catholic groups gained support among students, rural workers, and urban labor. After the Soccer War of 1969 (between Honduras and El Salvador), the left in El Salvador reorganized according to various revolutionary theories. Fraudulent elections throughout the 1970s bolstered support for revolutionary groups among the general populace, and the military (and paramilitary) became more violent in their reprisals against suspected leftist sympathizers. In Nicaragua, protests against the Somoza dictatorship increased in the late 1960s as Anastasio Somoza (son of the founder of the Somoza dynasty) made plans to assume the presidency. Though it was founded in 1961, the revolutionary Frente Sandinista de Liberación Nacional (FSLN; Sandinista Liberation Front), gained few members immediately after its 1961 organization. However, commitment to the idea of revolution surged following the devastating 1972 Managua earthquake and the subsequent misuse of relief funds by the Somoza regime. The 1978 murder of conservative opposition leader Pedro Joaquín Chamorro radicalized many Nicaraguans who had previously hesitated to support armed struggle. The product of a broad coalition of opposition forces, the revolution triumphed on July 19, 1979.

2. In 1932 the military brutally squelched a peasant uprising in what became known as la Matanza (the Massacre). Following this incident, the use of indigenous dress ceased almost completely because much of the government repression targeted members of indigenous communities.

3. *Cenizas* was published first in Spain in 1966, and its first Salvadoran publication came some ten years later.

4. For further perspectives on historical narrative, see White's *Figural Realism* (1999).

5. For her analysis of sexual oppression in the novels of Claribel Alegría, see Shea's *Women as Outsiders* (1993).

6. Late in 1931, Salvadoran General Maximiliano Hernández Martínez rescinded a promise to hold elections in January 1932. Sectors of the Salvadoran population had already begun to organize, seeking better economic conditions and the preservation of their cultures. When the promise of elections disappeared, the momentum for insurrection increased, and violence erupted. The military moved quickly to end the uprising, targeting the organized political opposition as well as campesinos and Indians. Although the specific figures vary widely, thousands of people, many of whom were not involved in the insurrection, died at the hands of the military in February 1932. For a brief but thorough description of events, see James Dunkerley's essay, "El Salvador since 1930," in *Central America since Independence.*

7. Central American novels of concientización include *Un día en la vida* (1980) by Manlio Argueta and *La mujer habitada* (1988) by Gioconda Belli.

8. *Campesino* is often translated as "peasant." More specifically, it refers to rural agricultural workers. Most campesinos practice subsistence farming on small plots of their own, or they are wage laborers for large landholders, or both. The term *obrero* (sometimes *trabajador*) generally refers to laborers in industrial or factory jobs.

9. Wolfgang Iser, associated with reader-response criticism in the 1970s, explains at length the idea of gaps in texts in his book *The Act of Reading* (1978).

10. Farabundo Martí was one of the leaders the 1932 uprising.

11. Please see Margarita Zamora's *Reading Columbus* (1993) for extensive treatment of gendering and discourse of Columbus's diaries.

12. The traditional bildungsroman had a male protagonist who confronted the society around him and gradually assumed his position in it.

Chapter 2

1. See Laura Barbas Rhoden, "El testimonio después de la victoria," *Confluencia* 14.2 (Spring 1999): 63–75.

2. Like Gabriel García Márquez's Macondo, Faguas is a fictionalized Latin American landscape.

3. Revolutionary activity increased in Nicaragua in the 1970s, especially following the 1972 earthquake, the aftermath of which revealed the level of

corruption of the Somoza regime. One of the most famous revolutionary actions of the decade was the 1974 December assault. As a group of wealthy partygoers celebrated in an exclusive Managua neighborhood, Sandinistas entered the home where the festivities were being held and took the group hostage. They demanded the release of Sandinista political prisoners and safe passage out of the country. When the Sandinista demands were met, the revolutionary movement gained unprecedented publicity and enjoyed an upsurge in popular support.

4. According to David Whisnant, the figure of Herrera was resurrected in the mid-1930s by Nicaraguan feminist Josefa Toledo de Aguerri, and she was subsequently appropriated as an example of valor during the Sandinista struggle (419).

5. The Black Legend originated in the age of colonialism when European rivals competed for overseas territories. Competing powers such as the Dutch and the English attributed to Spain a unique cruelty and depravity, highlighting the conquest of the New World and the Inquisition as emblematic of that depravity.

6. Luce Irigaray's famous work *This Sex Which Is Not One* is a good source for readers interested in her observations of gender, culture, and women's sexuality.

7. For feminist commentary on this tendency, see Rosario Castellanos's biting satire *El eterno femenino* (1974), a play about women's roles and "history" in Latin America.

8. The voice of the woman-as-mother also occurs in Belli's poetry, from her earliest poems collected in *El ojo de la mujer* to the more recent *Apogeo*.

9. In particular, *Waslala* recalls the life of poet José Coronel Urtecho and his wife María Kautz. In her afterword, Belli makes clear that the novel itself is a means to recuperate the memory of these individuals, both of whom figure prominently in the written and oral traditions of Nicaragua.

10. Though of a different literary genre, *El país bajo mi piel* also shares the same concern with centering and history. In this case, Belli weaves the story of her life and nation into one comprehensive work, rendering inextricable the personal and the political. For example, she recounts her experiences as Sandinista militant, in which she participated as political attaché in international delegations but still found herself fending off sexual advances. In articulating the struggle to reconcile her bourgeois past with a popular revolutionary movement, she traces the private, psychological dramas that are deeply imbricated in political conflicts. Throughout, she locates herself in moments of historical import and yet notes that as a woman she was often

divorced from them by the prejudices of others. Narrated between past triumphs and the present dislocations, Belli's memoirs search both for self and nation, ultimately reading as a defense of self-determination, passion, and hope.

Chapter 3

1. The title *La niña blanca y los pájaros sin pies* literally means "the white girl and the birds without feet." The reference is to indigenous perceptions of Catholic religious symbols during the time of the conquest. The "white girl" is the Virgin Mary; the birds without feet are the doves of the Holy Spirit, depicted in religious iconography without their feet visible.

2. The quote is from Neruda's collection *Veinte poemas de amor y una canción desesperada.*

3. On that date the triumphant, Sandinista-led opposition took possession of Managua and united in an enormous celebration of Somoza's defeat.

4. León Viejo is an abandoned colonial city in Nicaragua, located at the foot of the Momotombo volcano. The structures of León Viejo were destroyed in the early seventeenth century by earthquakes and frequent volcanic eruptions.

Chapter 4

1. The title of this chapter is taken from that of Walter Mignolo's book about coloniality and subaltern knowledges (2000).

2. *Desaparecido* literally means "disappeared" in Spanish. The term gained currency as a collective noun (and as a *transitive* verb) in the 1970s and 1980s to refer to victims of repressive regimes in Central America and the Southern Cone. In both regions, the military and paramilitary groups were implicated in disappearing, or abducting, suspected leftist sympathizers and other political enemies.

3. See, for instance, Hernan Cortés's *Cartas de relación,* texts addressed to the king, in which Cortés carefully constructs an image of himself as the diligent representative of the king's interest. Throughout (and especially in relating the conquest of the Aztec capital), he also suppresses the complaints

of the indigenous opposition, his own soldiers, and his Spanish rivals.

4. Oviedo's volumes offer several "interviews" with indigenous caciques.

5. The years immediately preceding the 1992 commemoration of the quincentennial of Columbus's voyage were filled not only with plans for official, state celebrations but also with counterdiscourses emphasizing the injustices that came in the wake of the European arrival and that persist in the present.

6. Compared to mineral-rich Mexico and Peru, Costa Rica (lit., Rich coast) proved a major disappointment for the Spanish colonizers. It lacked the wealth of other regions and did not have a centralized indigenous population to supply labor; far from the seat of government in Guatemala, it was perceived as a backwater. Its riches, as it has turned out, have been its fertile soil and biological diversity, neither of which was particularly valued during colonial times.

7. This use of metaphor is reminiscent of the discourse of Christopher Columbus in his *Diarios,* a strange narrative produced when the reality of the Other stretched to the limit the European capacities to name and contain.

8. Throughout Mesoamerica, the west is the cardinal direction associated with the afterlife of warriors. The belief is common in pre-Columbian indigenous cultures associated with Nahuatl and Mayan language groups.

9. The Central Valley (actually plateaus and valleys) is the coffee-growing heartland of Costa Rica, and members of the most prominent families of the region have long dominated national politics. The Atlantic coast is separated by mountainous terrain from the Central Valley and only recently has been connected to the capital by highway.

Bibliography

Aguilar, Rosario. *Colección primavera sonámbula.* 3 vols. Managua: Editora de Arte, 1999.

———. *The Lost Chronicles of Terra Firma.* Trans. Edward W. Hood. Fredonia, N.Y.: White Pine Press, 1997.

———. *La niña blanca y los pájaros sin pies.* Managua: Nueva Nicaragua, 1992.

———. *Siete relatos sobre el amor y la guerra.* San José: EDUCA, 1986.

Alegría, Claribel. *Album familiar.* San José: EDUCA, 1982.

———. "Una buena estrella: Entrevista con Claribel Alegría." Interview by Miguel Huezo Mixco. *Cultura* 77 (September-December 1996): 80–95.

———. *Despierta, mi bien, despierta.* San Salvador: UCA Editores, 1987.

Alegría, Claribel, and Darwin J. Flakoll. *Cenizas de Izalco.* 4th ed. San José: EDUCA, 1993.

———. *No me agarran viva: La mujer salvadoreña en lucha.* Mexico City: Ediciones Era, 1988.

Allende, Isabel. *La casa de los espíritus.* Buenos Aires: Editorial Sudamericana, 1985.

Ang, Ien. "On Not Speaking Chinese: Postmodern Ethnicity and the Politics of Diaspora." In *Feminism and Cultural Studies,* ed. Morag Shiach, 540–65. New York: Oxford University Press, 1999.

Arellano, Jorge Eduardo, ed. *El güegüense.* 8th ed. Managua: Ediciones Distribuidora Cultural, 1998.

Arenal, Electa, and Stacey Schlau, eds. Trans. Amanda Powell. *Untold Sisters: Hispanic Nuns in Their Own Works.* Albuquerque: University of New Mexico Press, 1989.

Argueta, Manlio. *Un día en la vida.* San Salvador: UCA Editores, 1980.

Arias, Arturo. "Conciencia de la palabra: Algunos rasgos de la nueva narrativa centroamericana." *Hispamérica* 21.61 (April 1992): 411–58.

———. "Descolonizando el conocimiento, reformando la textualidad: Repensando el papel de la narrativa centroamericana." *Revista de crítica literaria latinoamericana* 21.42 (1995): 73–86.

———. *Gestos ceremoniales: Narrativa centroamericana, 1960–1990.* Guatemala City: Artemis and Edinter, 1998.

———, ed. *The Rigoberta Menchú Controversy.* Minneapolis: University of Minnesota Press, 2001.

Bakhtin, M. M. *The Dialogic Imagination.* Ed. Michael Holquist. Trans. Caryl Emerson and Michael Holquist. Austin: University of Texas Press, 1981.

Baldovinos, Ricardo Roque and Roy Boland Osegueda, eds. *De la guerra a la paz: Perspectivas críticas sobre la literatura moderna centroamericana.* Melbourne: Antípodas, 2002.

Barrios de Chungara, Domitila. *"Si me permiten hablar . . .": Testimonio de Domitila, una mujer de las minas de Bolivia.* Ed. Moema Viezzer. Mexico City: Siglo Veintiuno Editores, 1978.

Belli, Gioconda. *Apogeo.* Managua: Anamá Ediciones, 1997.

———. *The Country under My Skin: A Memoir of Love and War.* Trans. Kristina Cordero with the author. New York: Knopf, 2002.

———. *De la costilla de Eva.* Managua: Editorial Nueva Nicaragua, 1987.

———. *La mujer habitada.* 12th ed. Tafalla, Navarre, Spain: Editorial Txalaparta, 1992.

———. *El ojo de la mujer.* Managua: Editorial Vanguardia, 1991.

———. *El país bajo mi piel: Memorias de amor y guerra.* Barcelona: Plaza y Janés Editores, 2001.

———. *Sobre la grama.* Managua: INDESA, 1974.

———. *Sofía de los presagios.* Managua: Anamá Ediciones, 1997.

———. *Waslala.* Managua: Anamá Ediciones, 1996.

Berrón, Linda. *El expediente.* San José: EDUCA, 1989.

———. *Olimpia: Drama en cuatro actos.* San José: Editorial Mujeres, 1998.

———, ed. *Relatos de mujeres: Antología de narradoras de Costa Rica.* San José: Editorial Mujeres, 1993.

Beverley, John. *Against Literature.* Minneapolis: University of Minnesota Press, 1993.

Beverley, John, and Marc Zimmerman. *Literature and Politics in the Central American Revolutions.* Austin: University of Texas Press, 1990.

Bhabha, Homi K. *The Location of Culture.* London: Routledge, 1994.

Boschetto-Sandoval, Sandra M., and Marcia Phillips McGowan, eds. *Claribel Alegría and Central American Literature.* Athens: Ohio University Center for International Studies, 1994.

Bulmer-Thomas, Victor. "Nicaragua since 1930." In *Central America since Independence,* ed. Leslie Bethell, 227–76. New York: Cambridge University Press, 1991.

Burgos-Debray, Elizabeth. *Me llamo Rigoberta Menchú y así me nació la conciencia.* México, Siglo XXI, 1985.

Buss, Helen M. "A Feminist Revision of New Historicism to Give Fuller Readings of Women's Private Writing." In *Inscribing the Daily,* ed. Suzanne L. Bunkers and Cynthia A. Huff, 86–103. Amherst: University of Massachusetts Press, 1996.

Cabezas, Omar. *La montaña es algo más que una inmensa estepa verde.* Managua: Nueva Nicaragua, 1982.

Calvo, Yadira. *Literatura, mujer, y sexismo.* San José: Editorial Costa Rica, 1984.

Carey-Webb, Allen. *Making Subject(s): Literature and the Emergence of National Identity.* New York: Garland Publishing, 1998.

Castellanos, Rosario. *El eterno femenino: Farsa.* Mexico City: Fondo de Cultura Económica, 1975.

Castellón, Blanca. *Ama del espíritu.* Managua: Editorial Decenio, 1995.

Castillo, Debra. *Talking Back: Toward a Latin American Feminist Literary Criticism.* Ithaca: Cornell University Press, 1992.

Castro, Amanda. *Poetry by Contemporary Honduran Women.* Trans. Amanda Castro and Margarita McNab. Lewiston, N.Y.: Edwin Mellen Press, 2002.

Chodorow, Nancy J. *Feminism and Psychoanalytic Theory.* New Haven: Yale University Press, 1989.

Cohen, Henry. "A Feminist Novel in Sandinista Nicaragua: Gioconda Belli's *La mujer habitada.*" *Discurso* 9.2 (1992): 37–48.

Craft, Linda J. *Novels of Testimony and Resistance from Central America.* Gainesville: University Press of Florida, 1997.

Darío, Rubén. *Azul.* 1888. Reprint, Bogotá: Panamericana Editorial, 1993.

Davin, Anna. "Redressing the Balance or Transforming the Art? The British Experience." In *Retrieving Women's History,* ed. S. Jay Kleinberg, 60–78. New York: UNESCO Press, 1988.

Derrida, Jacques. *Of Grammatology.* Trans. Gayatri Chakravorty Spivak. Baltimore: Johns Hopkins University Press, 1976.

Drake, Paul W. *Money Doctors, Foreign Debts, and Economic Reforms in Latin America from the 1890s to the Present.* Wilmington, Del.: Scholarly Resources, 1994.

Dunkerley, James. "El Salvador since 1930." In *Central America since Independence,* ed. Leslie Bethell, 159–90. Cambridge: Cambridge University Press, 1991.

Escudos, Jacinta. *Apuntes de una historia de amor que no fue.* San Salvador: UCA Editores, 1987.

———. *El desencanto.* San Salvador: Consejo Nacional para la Cultura y el Arte, 2001.

———. *Felicidad doméstica y otras cosas aterradoras.* Guatemala City: Editorial X, 2002.

Esquivel, Laura. *Como agua para chocolate.* Mexico City: Planeta, 1989.

Fallas, Carlos Luis. *Mamita Yunai.* 1941. Reprint, San José: Librería Lehmann, 1977.

Fernández de Oviedo y Valdés, Gonzálo. *Corónica de las Indias.* Salamanca: Junta, 1547.

Field, Les W. *The Grimace of the Macho Ratón: Artisans, Identity, and Nation in Late-Twentieth-Century Western Nicaragua.* Durham, N.C.: Duke University Press, 1999.

Franco, Jean. "Afterword: From Romance to Refractory Aesthetic." In *Latin American Women's Writing,* ed. Anny Brooksbank Jones and Catherine Davies, 226–37. New York: Clarendon Press, 1996.

———. "Going Public: Reinhabiting the Private." In *On Edge: The Crisis of Contemporary Latin American Culture,* ed. George Yúdice, Jean Franco, and Angel Flores, 65–83. Minneapolis: University of Minnesota Press, 1992.

———. "The Nation as Imagined Community." In *The New Historicism,* ed. H. Aram Veeser, 204–12. New York: Routledge, 1989.

———. *Plotting Women: Gender and Representation in Mexico.* New York: Columbia University Press, 1989.

Gamero de Medina, Lucila. *Blanca Olmedo.* 4th ed. Mexico City: Editorial Diana, 1972.

García Canclini, Néstor. *Hybrid Cultures.* Trans. Christopher L. Chiappari and Sylvia L. López. Minneapolis: University of Minnesota Press, 1995.

García Márquez, Gabriel. *Cien años de soledad.* Buenos Aires: Editorial Sudamericana, 1967.

———. *El otoño del patriarca.* Buenos Aires: Editorial Sudamericana, 1975.

Garma, Isabel. *El hoyito del perraje.* Guatemala: Ministerio de Cultura y Deportes, 1994.

Gohlman, Susan Ashley. *Starting Over: The Task of the Protagonist in the Contemporary Bildungsroman.* New York: Garland Publishing, 1990.

Gold, Janet. *Clementina Suárez: Her Life and Poetry.* Gainesville: University Press of Florida, 1995.

———, ed. *Volver a imaginarlas: retratos de escritoras centroamericanas.* Tegucigalpa: Editorial Guaymuras, 1998.

Gómez, Ana Ilce. *Las ceremonias del silencio.* 2d ed. Managua: Editorial Vanguardia, 1989.

González, Aníbal. "Modernismo y represión: Hacia una lectura psicoanalítica de los textos modernistas." *Siglo XX* 12.1–2 (1994): 129–44.

González, Ann. "'Las mujeres de mi país': An Introduction to the Feminist Fiction of Rosario Aguilar." *Revista/Review Interamericana* 23:1–2 (Spring-Summer 1993): 63–72.

Gramsci, Antonio. *Selections from the Prison Notebooks.* Ed. and trans. Quintin Hoare and Geoffrey Nowell-Smith. London: Lawrence and Wishart, 1971.

Gualtieri, Claudia. "The Colonial Exotic Deconstructed: A Suggested Reading Paradigm for Post-Colonial Texts." In *Nationalism vs. Internationalism: (Inter)national dimensions of literatures in English,* ed. Wolfgang Zach and Ken L. Goodwin. Tübingen: Stauffenburg Verlag, 1996.

Guardia, Gloria. *El último juego.* San José: EDUCA, 1977.

Gunn, Janet Varner. *Autobiography: Toward a Poetics of Experience.* Philadelphia: University of Pennsylvania Press, 1982.

Gutiérrez, Joaquín. *Murámonos, Federico: Novela.* San José: Editorial Costa Rica, 1973.

Hernández, Mildred. *Diario de cuerpos.* Guatemala: Editorial Oscar de León Palacios, 1998.

———. *Orígenes.* Guatemala: Editorial Oscar de León Palacios, 1995.

Higonnet, Margaret R. "Civil Wars and Sexual Territories." In *Arms and the Woman: War, Gender, and Literary Representation,* ed. Helen M. Cooper, Adrienne Auslander Munich, and Susan Merrill Squier, 80–96. Chapel Hill: University of North Carolina Press, 1989.

———. "New Cartographies, an Introduction." In *Reconfigured Spheres: Feminist Explorations of Literary Space,* ed. Margaret R. Higonnet and Joan Templeton, 1–19. Amherst: University of Massachusetts Press, 1994.

Hirsch, Marianne. *Mother/Daughter Plot: Narrative, Psychoanalysis, Feminism.* Bloomington: University of Indiana Press, 1989.

Hite, Molly. Foreword to *Redefining Autobiography in Twentieth-Century Women's Fiction,* ed. Janice Morgan and Colette T. Hall, xiii–xvi. New York: Garland Publishing, 1991.

Horton Reiss, Cheryl. "Awakenings: Oral and Written Discourse in *Despierta, mi bien, despierta.*" In *Claribel Alegría and Central American Literature,* ed. Sandra M. Boschetto-Sandoval and Marcia Phillips McGowan, 131–43. Athens: Ohio University Center for International Studies, 1994.

Irigaray, Luce. *This Sex Which Is Not One.* Trans. Catherine Porter and Carolyn Burke. Ithaca: Cornell University Press, 1985.

Isaacs, Jorge. *María.* Mexico City: Editorial Porrúa, 1994.

Iser, Wolfgang. *The Act of Reading.* Baltimore: Johns Hopkins University Press, 1978.

Istarú, Ana. *Baby Boom en el paraíso / Hombres en escabeche.* San José: Editorial Costa Rica, 2001.

Joyce, James. *Portrait of the Artist as a Young Man.* London: Egoist, 1917.

Kadir, Djelal. *The Other Writing: Postcolonial Essays in Latin America's Writing Culture.* West Lafayette, Ind.: Purdue University Press, 1993.

Kaminsky, Amy. "Entradas a la historia: *La mujer habitada.*" *Hispamérica* 23.67 (April 1994): 19–31.

Kristeva, Julia. *The Kristeva Reader.* Ed. Toril Moi. New York: Columbia University Press, 1986.

Lars, Claudia. *Canción redonda.* San José: Ediciones del Convivo, 1937.

———. *La casa de vidrio.* Santiago, Chile: Zig-Zag, 1942.

León-Portilla, Miguel. *La visión de los vencidos.* Mexico City: Universidad Nacional Autónoma, 1959.

Lerner, Gerda. *The Creation of Patriarchy.* New York: Oxford University Press, 1986.

———. *The Majority Finds Its Past.* New York: Oxford University Press, 1979.

Lloyd, David. "Violence and the Constitution of the Novel." *Meanjin* 51.4 (Summer 1992): 751–65.

Lobo, Tatiana. *El año del laberinto.* San José: Ediciones Farben, 2000.

———. *Asalto al paraíso.* San José: Editorial de la Universidad de Costa Rica, 1992.

———. *Calypso.* San José: Ediciones Farben, 1996.

———. *Entre Dios y el diablo.* San José: Editorial de la Universidad de Costa Rica, 1993.

———. *Tiempo de claveles.* San José: Editorial Costa Rica, 1990.

Lobo, Tatiana, and Mauricio Meléndez Obando. *Negros y blancos: Todo mezclado.* San José: Editorial de la Universidad de Costa Rica, 1997.

Lowe, Lisa, and David Lloyd. Introduction to *The Politics of Culture in the Shadow of Capital*, 1–32. Durham, N.C.: Duke University Press, 1997.

Lugones, María C., and Elizabeth V. Spelman. "Have We Got a Theory for You! Feminist Theory, Cultural Imperialism, and the Demand for 'the Woman's Voice.'" *Women's Studies International Forum* 6.6 (1983): 573–81.

March, Kathleen. "Gioconda Belli: The Erotic Politics of the Great Mother." *Monographic Review/Revista Monográfica* 6 (1990): 245–57.

Marchant, Elizabeth A. *Critical Acts: Latin American Women and Cultural Criticism.* Gainesville: University Press of Florida, 1999.

Marcus, George. "Contemporary Problems of Ethnography in the Modern World System." In *Writing Culture,* ed. James Clifford and George E. Marcus, 165–93. Berkeley: University of California Press, 1986.

Mastretta, Angeles. *Mal de amores.* Mexico City: Alfaguara, 1996.

Meneses, Vidaluz. *Llama en el aire.* Managua: Editorial Nueva Nicaragua, 1991.

Mignolo, Walter. *Local Histories/Global Designs.* Princeton: Princeton University Press, 2000.

Najlis, Michele. *Cantos de Ifigenia.* Managua: Editorial Vanguardia, 1991.

———. *El viento armado.* Guatemala City: Editorial Universitaria, 1969.

Naranjo, Carmen. *Ondina.* San José: EDUCA, 1983.

———. *Los perros no ladraron.* 2d ed. San José: EDUCA, 1974.

Odio, Eunice. *Territorio del alba y otros poemas.* San José: EDUCA, 1974.

———. *El tránsito de fuego.* San Salvador: Ministerio de Cultura, 1957.

Oreamuno, Yolanda. *La ruta de su evasión.* Guatemala: Ministerio de Educación Pública, 1949.

Ovares, Flora, Margarita Rojas, Carlos Santander, and María Elena Carballo, eds. *Casa paterna.* San José: Editorial de la Universidad de Costa Rica, 1993.

Palacios, Nidia. *Voces femeninas en la narrativa de Rosario Aguilar.* Managua: Editorial Ciencias Sociales, 1998.

Pedro, Valentín de. *Vida de Rubén Darío.* Buenos Aires: Los Libros del Mirasol, 1961.

Pellón, Gustavo. "The Spanish American Novel: Recent Developments, 1975–1990." In *The Cambridge History of Latin American Literature,* ed. Roberto González Echevarría and Enrique Pupo-Walker, 2:279–302. New York: Cambridge University Press, 1996.

Pineda de Gálvez, Adaluz, ed. *Honduras, mujer y poesía: Antología de la poesía hondureña escrita por mujeres, 1865–1998.* Tegucigalpa: Guardabarranco, 1998.

Pope, Randolph D. "The Spanish American Novel from 1950 to 1975." In *The Cambridge History of Latin American Literature,* ed. Roberto González Echevarría and Enrique Pupo-Walker, 2:226–78. New York: Cambridge University Press, 1996.

Pratt, Mary Louise. *Imperial Eyes: Travel Writing and Transculturation.* London: Routledge, 1992.

Prego, Irma. *Mensajes al más allá.* San José: EDUCA, 1987.

Ramos, Carmen. "The History of Women in Latin America." In *Retrieving Women's History: Changing Perceptions of the Role of Women in Politics and Society,* ed. S. Jay Kleinberg, 303–18. New York: UNESCO Press, 1988.

Rich, Adrienne. *Of Woman Born.* New York: Norton, 1976.

Richard, Nelly. *Masculino/femenino: Prácticas de la diferencia y cultura democrática.* Santiago, Chile: Francisco Zegers Editor, 1993.

Rodas, Ana María. *El fin de los mitos y los sueños.* Guatemala: RIN 78, 1984.

———. *Poemas de la izquierda erótica.* Guatemala City: Editorial Landívar, 1973.

Rodríguez, Ileana. *House/Garden/Nation: Space, Gender, and Ethnicity in Post-Colonial Latin American Literatures by Women.* Durham, N.C.: Duke University Press, 1994.

———. "Rethinking the Subaltern: Patterns and Places of Subalternity in the New Millennium." *Dispositio/n* 19.46 (1994): 13–25.

———. *Women, Guerrillas, and Love: Understanding War in Central America.* Trans. Ileana Rodríguez with Robert Carr. Minneapolis: University of Minnesota Press, 1996.

Rodríguez Sáenz, Eugenia, ed. *Entre silencios y voces.* San José: Centro Nacional para el Desarrollo de la Mujer y la Familia, 1997.

———. *Mujeres, género e historia en América Central durante los siglos XVIII, XIX y XX.* San José: Plumstock Mesoamerican Studies/ UNIFEM, 2002.

———. *Un siglo de luchas femeninas.* San José: Editorial de la Universidad de Costa Rica, 2002.

Rosowski, Susan J. "The Novel of Awakening." In *The Voyage In: Fictions of Female Development,* ed. Elizabeth Abel, Marianne Hirsch, and Elizabeth Langland, 49–68. Hanover: University Press of New England, 1983.

Ross, Yazmín. *La flota negra.* Mexico City: Alfaguara, 1999.

Rossi, Anacristina. *Limón blues.* Mexico City: Alfaguara, 2002.

———. *La loca de Gandoca.* San José: EDUCA, 1992.

Rowe, William, and Vivian Schelling. *Memory and Modernity.* London: Verso, 1991.

Sabonge, Aída Ondina. *Declaración doméstica.* Tegucigalpa: Editorial Universitaria, 1993.

Sahagún, Bernardino de. *General History of the Things of New Spain: Florentine Codex.* Santa Fe, N.M.: School of American Research, 1950–82.

Saporta Sternbach, Nancy. "Engendering the Future: *Ashes of Izalco* and the Making of a Writer." In *Claribel Alegría and Central American Literature,* ed. Sandra M. Boschetto-Sandoval and Marcia Phillips McGowan, 60–74. Athens: Ohio University Center for International Studies, 1994.

Scott, Joan Wallach. "The Problem of Invisibility." In *Retrieving Women's History,* ed. S. Jay Kleinberg, 5–29. New York: UNESCO Press, 1988.

Sefchovich, Sara. *La señora de los sueños.* Mexico City: Planeta, 1993.

Serrano, Marcela. *Antigua vida mía.* Santiago, Chile: Alfaguara, 1995.

Shea, Maureen. *Women as Outsiders: Undercurrents of Oppression in Latin American Literature.* San Francisco: Austin and Winfield, 1993.

Sommer, Doris. *Foundational Fictions.* Berkeley: University of California Press, 1991.

Souza, Raymond D. "Novel and Context in Costa Rica and Nicaragua." *Romance Quarterly* 33.4 (November 1996): 453–62.

Spivak, Gayatri. *Outside in the Teaching Machine.* New York: Routledge, 1993.

Stuurman, Siep. "In the Long Run We Shall All Be Dead." In *The Point of Theory: Practices of Cultural Analysis,* ed. Mieke Bal and Inge E. Boer, 125–37. New York: Continuum, 1994.

Suárez, Clementina. *Con mis versos saludo a las generaciones futuras.* Tegucigalpa: Ediciones Libreria Paradiso, 1988.

———. *Creciendo con la hierba.* San Salvador: n.p., 1957.

Tapscott, Stephen. *Twentieth-Century Latin American Poetry.* Austin: University of Texas Press, 1996.

Tiffin, Helen. "Post-Colonialism, Post-Modernism, and the Rehabilitation of Post-Colonial History." *Journal of Commonwealth Literature* 23.1 (1988): 169–81.

Toledo, Aída. *Realidad más extraña que el sueño.* Guatemala: Ministerio de Cultura y Deportes, 1994.

Toledo, Aída, and Anabella Acevedo Leal. *Tanta imagen tras la puerta.* Guatemala: Universidad Rafael Landívar, 1999.

Treacy, Mary Jane. "Creation of the Woman Warrior: Claribel Alegría's *They Won't Take Me Alive.*" In *Claribel Alegría and Central American Literature,* ed. Sandra M. Boschetto-Sandoval and Marcia Phillips McGowan, 75–96. Athens: Ohio University Press, 1994.

Vallbona, Rima de. *Noche en vela.* San José: EDUCA, 1968.

Vanegas, Juan de Dios, and Alfonso Valle. *Nacimiento y primera infancia de Rubén Darío.* Managua: Ediciones del Club del Libro Nicaragüense, 1962.

Whisnant, David. *Rascally Signs in Sacred Places.* Chapel Hill: University of North Carolina Press, 1995.

White, Hayden. *Figural Realism.* Baltimore: Johns Hopkins University Press, 1999.

———. "Storytelling: Historical and Ideological." In *Centuries' Ends, Narrative Means,* ed. Robert Newman, 58–78. Stanford, Calif.: Stanford University Press, 1996.

Williams, Robert G. *States and Social Evolution.* Chapel Hill: University of North Carolina Press, 1994.

Willis, Susan. "Histories, Community, and Sometimes Utopia." In *Feminisms,* ed. Robyn R. Warhol and Diane Price Herndl, 815–29. New Brunswick, N.J.: Rutgers University Press, 1991.

Woodward, Ralph Lee. *Central America: A Nation Divided.* 2d ed. New York: Oxford University Press, 1985.

Yalom, Marilyn. *Maternity, Mortality, and the Literature of Madness.* University Park: Pennsylvania State University Press, 1985.

Young, Robert J. C. *Colonial Desire.* London: Routledge, 1995.

Zamora, Daisy. *A cada quien la vida.* Managua: Editorial Vanguardia, 1994.

———. *La violenta espuma.* Managua: Ministerio de Cultura, 1981.

———, ed. *Mujer nicaragüense en la poesía.* Editorial Nueva Nicaragua, 1992.

Zamora, Margarita. *Reading Columbus.* Berkeley: University of California Press, 1993.

Index